# HIT

# CLASSICS IN WOMEN'S STUDIES SERIES

Jane Addams, Emily G. Balch, and Alice Hamilton,
*Women at The Hague*

Matilda Joslyn Gage, *Woman, Church and State*

Charlotte Perkins Gilman, *The Man-Made World*

Margaret Sanger, *The Pivot of Civilization*

Elizabeth Cady Stanton, *Eighty Years and More*

Mary E. Walker, MD, *Hit: Essays on Women's Rights*

# HIT

## ESSAYS ON WOMEN'S RIGHTS

# MARY E. WALKER, M.D.

### WITH AN INTRODUCTION BY
## MERCEDES GRAF

CLASSICS IN WOMEN'S STUDIES

**Humanities Press**

ROWMAN & LITTLEFIELD
*Lanham • Boulder • New York • London*

Published by Rowman & Littlefield
An imprint of The Rowman & Littlefield Publishing Group, Inc.
4501 Forbes Boulevard, Suite 200, Lanham, Maryland 20706
www.rowman.com

86-90 Paul Street, London EC2A 4NE, United Kingdom

British Library Cataloguing in Publication Information Available

**Library of Congress Cataloging-in-Publication Data**

The Humanities Press edition of this book was previously catalogued by the
Library of Congress as follows:

Walker, Mary Edwards, 1832–1919.
 Hit : essays on women's rights / by Mary E. Walker ; with an introd. by
Mercedes Graf.
  p. cm.—(Classics in women's studies series)
 Originally published: New York : American News Co., 1871.
 Includes bibliographical references.
 ISBN 1–59102–098–0 (paper)
 1. Social problems. 2. Women's rights. 3. Women—Social conditions.
I. Title. II. Classics in women's studies.


HN64.W18 2003
305.42—dc21
                                                          2003050838

ISBN 9781538179611 (cloth) | ISBN 9781538178331 (pbk.) | ISBN
9781538178348 (epub)

MARY EDWARDS WALKER, American physican and reformer, was born on November 26, 1832, near Oswego, New York. Her father was a country doctor and freethinker who supported women's education and rights, and dress reform. Mary also became an advocate of women's rights and espoused dress reform, discarding the restrictive women's clothing of the day in favor of bloomers and later, men's clothing.

In June 1855 Walker, the only woman in her class, graduated from Syracuse Medical College in New York, joining the few women doctors in the nation. In 1856 she married physician Albert Miller, retaining her own name. They established a joint medical practice in Rome, New York, but the practice floundered due to the public's reluctance to accept a woman physician. They divorced in 1869.

At the outbreak of the Civil War, Walker tried to enlist in the Union army. Refused a commission as a medical officer, she volunteered as an acting assistant surgeon, the first female surgeon in the U.S. Army. She first worked in the U.S. Patent Office Hospital in Washington and then as a field surgeon near the Union front lines.

Walker was finally appointed assistant surgeon in the Army of the Cumberland in September 1863. She was then appointed assistant surgeon of the Fifty-second Ohio Infantry. In 1864 she was taken prisoner by Confederate troops and imprisoned in Richmond, Virginia, until she was returned to the Fifty-second Ohio during a prisoner exchange. She then spent the rest of the war practicing at a Louisville, Kentucky, female hospital and at an orphan's asylum in Tennessee.

On November 11, 1865, President Andrew Johnson signed a bill to present Walker with the Congressional Medal of Honor for Meritorious Service, in recognition of her war efforts even though she never officially obtained an army commission. She was the only woman ever to receive the nation's highest military award.

After the war, Walker became a writer and lecturer, touring here and abroad on women's rights, dress reform, health, and temperance issues. She was elected president of the National Dress Reform Association  in 1866 and was arrested numerous times for wearing full male dress. She wrote a combination biography and commentary called *Hit* and a second work, *Unmasked, or the Science of Immortality*.

In 1917 Walker's Congressional Medal (along with the medals of 910 others) was taken away when Congress revised the Medal of Honor standards to include only "actual combat with an enemy." Walker refused to return her medal, wearing it every day until her death in Oswego on February 21, 1919.

In 1977 an army board reinstated her medal posthumously, citing her "distinguished gallantry, self-sacrifice, patriotism, dedication, and unflinching loyalty to her country, despite the apparent discrimination because of her sex."

# INTRODUCTION

In the history of the United States, more than three thousand Medals of Honor have been awarded, but only one has gone to a woman—Dr. Mary Edwards Walker. Born on November 26, 1832, in Oswego, New York, she was only twenty-eight years old when she first volunteered her services in a makeshift hospital in the United States Patent Office in Washington, D.C.[1] A short time later, she became the only woman to be awarded a contract as an acting assistant surgeon in the Civil War and the only female physician taken as a prisoner of war and exchanged for a Confederate officer.[2] Years later when she was asked how she had earned her medal she replied: "The special valor, was for going into the enemy's grounds, when the inhabitants were suffering for professional service, and sent to our lines to beg assistance, and no man surgeon was willing to respond, for fear of being taken prisoner."[3]

Walker's words leave no doubt as to her attitude toward men—most certainly, they were not superior to women. This is one of the messages she hoped to get across to the public in 1870 when she wrote her book *Hit*, which can be considered an autobiographical account.[4] No one is quite sure what the title means, although it seems likely that she wrote it hoping her words would "hit" their mark. Because Walker chose not to explain its meaning to her readers, we shall never know for certain. As far as her contemporaries were concerned, the title appeared to be as puzzling as Walker's lifestyle, which was dominated by her insistence on wearing male attire.

When she had started studying medicine at Syracuse Medical College in December of 1853, for example, Walker began to experiment with wearing clothes that were more practical for her profession.[5] She began by shortening her skirts and ended up with adopting the bloomer style of dress. At her marriage in 1856 to Dr. Arthur Miller, a classmate, she appeared in trousers and a dress-coat. During the Civil War, and after an unhappy marriage, she could be seen on the battlefield wearing her version of the Federal uniform, a long coat over pants; and more often than not, she tied the green surgeon's sash around her waist as well. When the war ended, Walker could be found marching across the country delivering lectures on women's rights and dress reform, now wearing modified male attire—a black suit that consisted of a dress drawn in at the waist and reaching a little below the knee under which were worn loose-fitting trousers.[6]

Throughout her lifetime, Walker continued to stress the right to choose her own clothes even though she was arrested on several occasions from 1866 to 1913 for masquerading as a man in public.[7] Having rejected gender constraints in her choice of a profession that was dominated by males, she was just as willing to reject the accepted standard woman's dress. For society at that time, wearing trousers was equated with maleness, and this in turn represented the male prerogatives associated with freedom and independence. In fact, Walker stated: "Everything that makes woman in any degree independent of man, and, as a consequence, independent of marriage for support, is frowned down by a certain class of individuals." Her insistence on donning trousers was seen as a renunciation of all that was feminine, and consequently her behavior was viewed as a reaction against the natural social order. Imbued with her reform ideas, however, Walker was just as determined to oppose convention, and she contended that "the time is coming when every woman will dress in this style, for the advantages are too evident, to be much longer overlooked." And, of course, pants eventually became an everyday occurrence during World War I when women abandoned their skirts for trousers.

When people questioned Walker as to why she wore pants in the face of such strong public opinion, she explained that long skirts were not only uncomfortable, but also unsanitary. "It is a well known fact," she stated, "[that] Dress Reform for women is of paramount importance." While she did not require that other women adopt her attire, she extolled its benefits, and in *Hit* she devoted a chapter to explaining her views on dress reform. "Few young women are to be found," she pointed out, "that are fit for marriage, because they have been dressed in such a manner that weakness if not mechanical displacements have resulted." Long dresses and corsets did not allow for freedom of motion, hoops caused problems when walking against the wind, and the snug fit at the waist interfered with digestion and circulation. She also criticized the tight elastic bands that were used to hold up stockings since they compressed the muscles of the leg, and she opposed the fashionable shoes with their high heels that thrust the body forward in the wrong position so as to contort the whole frame. Exaggerated hairstyles and tight braiding could also cause harm to the head and scalp. Perhaps this was part of the reason why Walker preferred to wear her dark brown hair in loose curls. While she preferred the male style of dress, she was very proud of the long ringlets that left no doubt as to her true gender.[8]

Although Walker was outspoken in pointing to a connection between fashionable dress and female ill health, she was in a unique position to speak on such matters as she was only one of approximately two hundred medical women in the country at the time. She also believed that female doctors had a special contribution to make to the profession, a belief that was reinforced in the popular health manuals of the period that promoted the idea of women as natural healers. As further proof of her views, she had taken a special course of studies in March of 1862 at the Hygeia Therapeutic College, an unconventional water-cure medical school. Here prevention rather than cure was stressed, and she studied natural cures as contrasted with the heroic and often harsh methods like bloodletting, leeches, cathartics, and emetics.

At the same time, Walker believed that women were in the process of creating new roles for themselves and that dress reform was the symbol of their new status in a society in which they were expected to perform these increasingly difficult tasks in family life. Furthermore, since a woman's procreative role often made her health more precarious than her mate's, Walker stressed the importance of the state of female health and its importance for the family. She urged women to consider that "Nothing but a thoroughly hygienic Dress, worn all through young girlhood, womanhood, and wifehood will save the vitality of women for the various duties of life, and especially for the high duties of a maternity that shall do the greatest credit to herself and her children." In keeping with this, she opposed "the wretched manner in which little children are dressed," noting that in the year 1860 alone "300,000 deaths occurred before the age of five years!"

She was further convinced that women should share their common concerns and unite together for the greater good. This kind of collective sensitivity to the community among women was symbolized in the reform literature with its many references to the "sisterhood." Clearly Walker demonstrated this was the case for her dedication

following the title page of *Hit* reads: "To that Great Sisterhood . . . I dedicate this work in hope that it will contribute to right your wrongs, lighten your burdens and
increase your self-respect and self-reliance, and place in
your hands that power which shall emancipate you from
the bondage of all that is oppressive."

Of the eight chapters in *Hit*, two of them are concerned with the subjects of divorce, and love and marriage.
Here the reader sees many personal references to Walker's
former married state, especially to the philandering of Dr.
Miller that ultimately led to their divorce. "There must be
stability in the affections," she emphasized, "or there can be
no true Love." In his defense, it should be noted that the
young husband indulged his bride when she insisted the
word "obey" be omitted from the ceremony and that she
be permitted to retain her last name. When they started to
practice medicine together, the new bride preferred to
hyphenate her name, referring to herself as "Dr. Miller-
Walker." In her book, she defended a woman's right to
choose how she would be called, stating that the time was
not far off when each person "will keep their own names
when they marry." Walker further maintained that if a
woman must be called "Mrs." to let the world know she
was married, "why not call a man Misterer for the purpose
of enlightening the world as to his condition?"

All in all, Walker believed in marriage even though she
had failed in this most important of all endeavors. Yet she
must have been wounded deeply, because she stressed the
fact that thousands of women have been accused of jeal-

ousy after being deceived by their spouses when they are really "sorrowing over a husband's infidelity." Years later, in fact, Walker refused to talk about Dr. Miller at all even with close friends and relatives, and many outsiders who were critical of her believed she was a disappointed spinster since she had resorted to using only her maiden name before the start of the Civil War.

Disappointments in her personal life did not stop Walker from being a crusader, and in *Hit* she devoted two chapters to addressing the evils of tobacco and alcohol. She was a zealous advocate for public health and social reform, as were many of her sister health reformers, and she expressed this by pointing out the relationship between science and the everyday life of women and the family. Thus, alcohol and tobacco were injurious to health and they would undoubtedly "poison the happiness of domestic life." She urged smokers to consider the effects of the "fumes" on others, and she reiterated that as far as the members of the family were concerned: "Tobacco cannot be used in any form, without producing evil effects, mentally or physically, sooner or later, upon the user, the wife and the children." In many ways, Walker's ideas were advanced for a woman of her time although we now know about the secondhand effects of cigarette smoke today. Yet some of her charges against "the poison" seemed so exaggerated and outrageous that many people could only scoff at the diminutive figure in pants or shake their heads in disbelief.[9] It was hard to accept the fact, for instance, that tobacco often produced "not only paralysis, but insanity."

Walker preached against alcohol and its physical and psychological effects, especially delirium tremens, apoplexy, or softening of the brain—symptoms that can be associated today with a medical condition known as Korsakov Psychosis or chronic alcoholic delirium. The physical and emotional abuse that an alcoholic might inflict on his family was also apparent to her, and she recounted stories in which husbands had killed their wives or injured their children while intoxicated. She concluded that "neither pen nor brush can ever do justice to the subject in portraying the real condition of families, where the intoxicating cup has found an honored place."

An advocate of temperance, Walker could not understand why the government allowed the poison to be made and licenses sold for its distribution. (In this regard, she predicted what would happen with Prohibition.) While she maintained that men were the perpetuators of evil drink, women did not escape her condemnation either. In her book, she proclaimed: "It is rare indeed to find a woman who is lost to all moral sense that does not tip the bottle."[10] Of course, this statement was probably intended to be a social indictment against those females who had betrayed their own sex by not upholding the moral superiority of women. No doubt, Walker contrasted this example with her own lifestyle and that of other women doctors.

For women who pursued medicine in the nineteenth century, religious perfectionism was a guiding force in their lives, and Walker was no exception.[11] She was convinced that both sexes had a moral and religious obligation

to society although it was the women who were more inclined as a group to demonstrate their religious piety by
contributing to the community welfare. Walker, for example, had contemplated medicine at one point so she
could enter the missionary field, and one of her most cherished possessions was a Bible that the chaplain had presented to her when she was incarcerated at Castle Thunder
in Richmond during the war. She made it clear in *Hit*,
however, that she had grown to have a much broader
interpretation of religious activity stating that "there is
something good in all religious beliefs," and advocating
that the Golden Rule be applied in everyday life. On the
other hand, Walker did not believe that church affiliation
for women was important unless they were elevated to
their true positions, as companions of men. "Any Religion
that gives the wife a servile position," she stressed, "is
beneath the great plans of Deity."

In her reflections on labor, we see evidence of a stance
that was consistent with the position of nineteenth-cen-
tury feminists who focused their agenda on equal opportunity while they struggled hard for women's right to work
in the public sphere. While Walker urged wives to help
their husbands, she dwelled on the plight of women who
needed to work outside the home, and she demanded
equal pay for the same kind of labor. She also believed that
work was essential to happiness and that no kind of work
"should be despised." In regard to the latter, Walker certainly knew what she was talking about. In her own lifetime, she had periods of financial stress because she could

not actively engage in the practice of medicine due to the problems she experienced with her eyes following her capture and imprisonment. When a professional agency suggested she give lectures in a tour of sideshows and dime museums in the Midwest at a fee of $150 per week, she accepted. One newspaper reporter commented harshly, "there was a time when this remarkable woman stood upon the same platform with Presidents and the world's greatest women. There is something grotesque in her appearance [now] on a stage built for freaks."[12]

Knowing the hardships that went along with being single in a society where few women had identities of their own, Walker was able to understand the expectations that were placed upon "refined" women. Single or married, they could not escape the demands society made on them. In an age when the cult of "domesticity" ruled, women were judged to be inferior to men, and they were told that true happiness would come from being the helpmates of their husbands and good mothers to their children. The ultimate figures of domestic self-sacrifice, they ruled their domestic spheres from the pedestals upon which society had placed them. Such was the tradition that Walker was writing against in *Hit* when she urged, of all things, that men should assist with the housework. "How much lighter would the broom and smoothing-irons seem," she emphasized, "if women knew that they had been used by men who had left a touch of appreciation upon them." And many a tired mother must have smiled when she read Walker's recommendation that even the sons of the household should be brought up to learn the complicated duties of housekeeping.

In her discussion of labor, Walker called for a greater recognition of the importance of work in raising the standard of living. Although it was obvious to her that both sexes were overworked, the condition of "laboring women" was made unbearable because of the pittance they were paid. In her mind, the situation for women was worsened by the fact that females had to marry out of necessity, whereas if they earned good pay for equal work they would be able to support themselves happily until a "really congenial" man was at hand. Still, as a physician she recognized that overwork was harmful mentally and physically. "No individuals can be entirely absorbed in excessive physical toil," she stated, "without detracting from the mental powers." Negative effects would also impact the children of overworked parents, for how could the minds of these youngsters be thoroughly developed if mothers and fathers had neither the time nor the opportunities to enrich their lives? Over a hundred years later, child advocates are still asking the same question, which is further proof of the kind of vision Walker had regarding the importance of the family and its influence.

But her enlightened views extended into other areas as well for she recognized that increased urbanization brought crowded and unsanitary living conditions. Walker felt that one remedy for this problem was to see that all persons had a home of their own. In fact, she admitted that she was ashamed that thousands of people toiled all their lives and died without ever owning one. The particular situation of women in this regard could not be overlooked either as there were few avocations where females could be paid enough money to enable them to purchase their own house. Another issue close to Walker's heart was woman's enfranchisement. She opposed those who reasoned that women had no right to vote because "they cannot be warriors and defend a country, and therefore have no right to take part in a government." She acknowledged several women figures in history who had won renown on the battlefield, but she did not include her name among them. It is surprising that she never mentioned her own experiences with the Union army since her struggle was conducted in the military establishment, arguably the most male of institutions. She had also volunteered at Fredericksburg and then at Chattanooga as the wounded streamed in from Chickamauga. Furthermore, her war work had been a popular topic on the lecture circuit in the United States and abroad, especially when presented by an attractive young female doctor clad in a male costume with the Medal of Honor pinned to her chest. While many people over the years criticized Walker for being egocentric and labeled her as arrogant, her omission in *Hit* regarding her own record of achievement speaks to the contrary. Here was a perfect opportunity to laud her own accomplishments, but she chose to ignore it.

One thing Walker would not ignore, however, was the chance to let men know her feelings about political equality. Toward the end of the chapter on woman's franchise, she addressed herself to her male readers, and launched into a strong attack on behalf of women every-where who were denied the vote. "Men of America," she declared, "you have robbed us of our most precious inher-itance. Through the power of brute force I see the ballot in your hands, but through the telescope of *justice* I see *woman* having it, is equally certain." Walker closed her remarks with the prediction that when the time came when women held the ballot in their hands, her beloved America would "be a whole Republic in reality, instead of being scarcely a *half* one." This last sentence summed up one of the main forces in her life, her patriotism and love of country.[13]

When death finally claimed Walker on February 21, 1919, at eighty-six years of age, she was buried in a black frock suit. Only the American flag draped over the casket sig-nified anything special about the woman who lay inside. Just a few people attended Walker's funeral as the popularity she had garnered in her active years waned as she grew older. A new generation neither knew or cared about the health reformer and suffragette who had stunned an army depart-ment with her demand to be accepted as a surgeon. But three things are certain: She lived long enough to see the women in her state be given the right to vote although national suf-frage was not achieved for some years after her death, and she witnessed the coming of Prohibition. Finally, she looked on as the women of the nation donned their trousers.

Looking back over her life, it can be said that Walker was light-years ahead of many of her colleagues in her views although she was often judged harshly for her dress and ideas that often seemed to fly in the face of common sense and tradition. Although it took a woman of exceptional determination and perseverance to risk public ridicule by advocating such ideas at a time when conventionality ruled, early postwar historians have tended to overlook Walker's real contributions because they could find no legitimate place for her in the official record of women's work in the Civil War. Walker's book deserves to be read today, however, as it puts into historical perspective the efforts of one of the first suffragists of America whose ideas helped promote the cause of the women's rights movement. On another level, it should also be perused as it gives us insights into the character of an early woman pioneer in medicine whose exploits generated a great deal of controversy given that they were so much at odds with the dominant image of the Victorian woman at the time. As much as Walker might have wanted to be recognized as one of the leading reformers of her day, however, she will probably be best remembered for paving the way for female physicians in the military as well as being the only woman up to now who has been awarded the Medal of Honor.

On the frontispiece of *Hit*, several quotes stand out under the title. The first one proclaims: "We live in deeds, not years." There could be no better epitaph for a bold crusader who devoted herself to so many worthy causes.

Mercedes Graf
Professor of Psychology
Governors State University
University Park, Illinois

# NOTES

1. She was actually born in a house on Bunker Hill Road in Oswego Town, New York, just a few miles outside of Oswego at the time. For more information about her life, see: Charles McCool Snyder, *Dr. Mary Walker, The Little Lady in Pants* (New York, 1977); Lida Poynter, "Dr. Mary Walker, The Forgotten Woman," manuscript in the Lida Poynter Papers, Archives and Special Collections on Women in Medicine, MCP Hahnemann University, Philadelphia, Pennsylvania.

2. Walker was awarded her contract on October 5, 1864, although she was never awarded a much-coveted army commission. She did not know that another female surgeon, Dr. Sarah Ann Chadwick Clapp, had volunteered as an assistant surgeon with the Seventh Illinois Cavalry (although she never received an official contract). While on an expedition, Walker was captured by Confederate sentries on April 10, 1864. For an account of Walker's war years see: Mercedes Graf, *A Woman of Honor: Dr. Mary E. Walker and the Civil War* (Gettysburg, Penn.: Thomas Publications, 2001).

3. "Letter of Mary E. Walker to the Honorable Adjutant General," dated April 22, 1916, Records of the War Department, Office of the Adjutant General, Records Group #94, Re: Dr. Mary Walker, National Archives and Record Administration, Washington, D.C. (Unless otherwise noted, all other quotes are from *Hit*). The medal was later rescinded on January 17, 1917, because she had not received it for action "involving actual conflict with an enemy, by gallantry or intrepidity, at the risk of life, above and beyond the call of duty." It was reinstated on June 10, 1977.

4. Walker wrote a second book seven years later: *Unmasked,*

*or the Science of Immorality.* She had planned to write an autobiography, but she never found the time to do so. Only thirty-eight pages of notes exist about her Civil War services that are entitled "Incidents Connected with the Army," and these are housed at Syracuse University Library, Department of Special Collections. Other papers and photos related to her life can be found at the Oswego County Historical Society, Oswego, New York.

5. Walker had just turned twenty-one years old when she began her studies.

6. The reform dress was slightly more tailored than the Bloomer costume. In later years, Walker adopted male attire almost completely and dressed in a men's suit with its frock coat and trousers, often even wearing a top hat in public.

7. It was a crime in those days to impersonate a man.

8. During the war she sacrificed her curls, as short hair was more practical on the battlefield. In 1982 Walker's portrait appeared on a new twenty-cent U.S. commemorative stamp, and she was pictured in a dress (of which she would have disapproved) with cascading curls.

9. Mary stood barely five feet tall. When she was released from her four months' confinement as a POW from Castle Thunder (a political prison on Cary Street), her niece reported that Walker weighed only about sixty pounds due to the privations she had endured. No doubt this was an exaggeration although medical reports indicate that it is common for POWs to suffer severe weight losses.

10. This might be construed as a veiled reference to her service (winter/spring of 1864/1865) as the Surgeon-in-Charge of the Louisville Female Military Prison that housed female rebel prisoners. Before her arrival, the place had been described "as no better than a brothel."

11. Although she was brought up a Methodist, she severed ties with this group and she chose a Unitarian minister to perform her marriage ceremony.

12. *Toledo Blade*, March 25, 1893. (She was sixty-one years old at that time.) Also see "Dr. Walker's New Role (in Dime Museum in Philadelphia)," *New York Times*, March 8, 1887; R. Werlich, "From Union Army Surgeon to Side Show Freak," *Civil War Times Illustrated* 6, no. 3 (1967): 46-50.

13. When Walker was at Castle Thunder, passers-by recalled that she used to sit by an open window waving a small flag out of it. On another occasion, she avowed: "Congress should assign women to duty in the Army with compensation, as well as colored men, averring that patriotism has no sex." Quoted in Poynter, "Dr. Mary Walker, The Forgotten Woman," p. 70.

Mary E. Walker M.D.

"We live in deeds, not years."

★   ★   ★   ★   ★

"They most live who think most,
Feel the noblest, act the best."

"Strength and wisdom only flower
When we toil for all our kind."

TO

*MY PARENTS;*

*And also*

*TO THE*

*PRACTICAL DRESS REFORMERS,*

The truest friends of humanity, who have done more for the universal elevation of woman in the past dozen years, than all others combined. You, who have *lived* the precepts and principles that others have only *talked*—who have been so consistent in your ideas of the equality of the sexes, by dressing in a manner to fit you for the duties of a noble and useful life. You, who have written and spoken, and been living martyrs to the all-important principles involved in a thoroughly hygienic dress, and thus given to the world an indisputable proof of your unflinching integrity. To You, in a word, who are the greatest philanthropists of the age, this second Dedication is made.

*And also*

*TO MY*

*PROFESSIONAL SISTERS,*

Of whatever School or Pathy, and all women who are laboring for the public good in any capacity.

*And lastly,*

*TO THAT*

*GREAT SISTERHOOD,*

Which embraces women with their thousand unwritten trials and sorrows, that God has not given to men the power to comprehend, I dedicate this work, in hope that it will contribute to right your wrongs, lighten your burdens and increase your self-respect and self-reliance, and place in your hands that power which shall emancipate you from the bondage of all that is oppressive.

# PREFACE

*"My words I give unto you."*

In presenting my book to the public, I have only to say, that a combination of motives, some of which have been the incentives in most other persons, have induced me to wield the thought-sender.

Were I to delay its publication until I had "fashioned it to the taste of the critics," thousands of women would suffer agonies in the waiting, that will gladly accept it in its imperfect condition, and rejoice that there are hearts that think of them in the silent hours when none but the great Sympathizer listens to the earnest prayer for strength. I make no pretensions that I have said *everything* that may be said upon the interesting subject of Marriage, or that what

I *have* said, is entirely new, or purely original; I have used my own language, and express my ideas in my own way, without attempting to exhaust the subject, which has claimed the attention of every human being to some *extent*, in some period of their life, if that life has been matured.

If the reader is induced to think calmly and reason profoundly on this important subject, I shall feel that much has been accomplished in the social world. I launch my frail barque into the stormy and fathomless sea of critics, prepared for whatever is to be. I shall be as pleased with the appreciation of a generous public as most persons. In cases where I shall be treated severely, I shall be consoled with the thought, that the *critics are earning their bread*, and that they are more capable of displaying their talents in "unkind cuts," than in culling what little of merit it may possess.

As to *myself*, the "good time coming" has not yet arrived, when an individual can speak of the little personal pronoun *I*, without being gravely charged with the criminal offence of *egotism*, notwithstanding the fact, that one is better acquainted with said pronoun than others can be, however extensive the acquaintance may have been. But next to self, is the Phrenologist.

The following was given by S. R. Wells, of the Phrenological Journal, 389 Broadway, N. Y.


MARY E. WALKER.


You should be known especially for your great activity, energy and executiveness; also for faith, hope, and trust, in

Providence; next, for your firmness, decision and self reliance; next, for your powers of observation and reflection.

You are both a good *looker* and a good *thinker.* You remember all that you *see,* distinctly, as well as your thoughts and experiences. Names, dates and minor details, may escape you, but facts, principles and important details, *never.*

You should also be known for your kindness, sympathy, and willingness to make personal sacrifices for the benefit of others; also for your constructiveness, planning power, and even for your inventive genius. You are full of resources; failing in one thing, you readily try another and another, till you ensure success.

You should also be known for your ability to endure privations. You could get along without food or sleep longer than most persons, and hold up under hardships; indeed, you are adapted to emergencies, and would excel in any hospital or prison services. Educated for it, you would be able even to perform surgical operations without flinching or fainting.

You may appreciate property and know its worth, but you want it simply to use, and not to *hoard.* You could not be wasteful, though you may sometimes be *generous* to a fault, but you are probably known for economy, for mechanical ingenuity, for prophetic forecast, for intellect, stability, force of character and propelling power.

It would be natural for you to desire all the rights and privileges, at least all the opportunities enjoyed by the other sex, that you could go the world over, acquiring knowledge and applying it in all directions.

You have much of the missionary spirit; the desire to do good, and confer favors on all you meet and you should be no *less* known for integrity, and true sense of justice, and a desire to do *right* under all circumstances.

You are naturally religiously disposed, though your views would be *broad* and *liberal*, not *narrow* or *sectarian*, nor are you superstitious or bigoted. You would worship God under all *circumstances*, and express gratitude for all things. If disappointed, you regard it simply as a blessing in disguise, and make the least of your trials, instead of the most of them.

In temper; you hold no malice, encourage no vindictive feeling, but you rather *forget* and *forgive* an injury, than punish the offender; still you would be a stickler for *justice*, and would insist on right and justice being *done* in all cases.

Socially, you are *warm-hearted* and *loving*, and though you deny yourself the pleasures of the social circle, you are always happiest when surrounded by those you love. If suitably mated, you would be happy as a wife. If a *mother*, you would be very kind and indulgent to children. As a *friend*, you would be always true, *standing by* those who are worthy, even in the most trying circumstances, and would almost sacrifice yourself on the altar of your friendships.

The love for *home*, is the same, though you can make yourself almost at home everywhere. The love for home and for friends may be called as strong as that for kindred. Because one was born in the same family, or bears the same name, it does not make him nearer to you than others.

Although cautious, watchful, guarded and mindful of

danger, you are free from timidity, and have not that shrinking, hesitating feeling, that declines responsibility, but on the contrary, where *duty* calls, there you go without regard to consequences; but you would not be reckless, heedless, nor even *careless*, but would be *prudent*, as a general thing; and though you would drive a fast horse, you would hold a stiff line, and steer your course with both judgment and cautiousness.

You have great tenacity of life, and would *hold on* when others would *let go*. Your recuperative powers are the same; a little rest, simple food and repose, puts you all right again, after great exposure. The appetite is good, and you enjoy the luxuries of the table, but you eat to live, rather than live to eat.

You are naturally extremely sensitive to blame or praise, nor would you be likely to do anything which would let you down, either in your own estimation, or in the estimation of others: still you hold yourself accountable to *Heaven* rather than to *persons*, and when you think yourself in the *right*, you pursue a straightforward course, without regard to what may be thought or said of you.

You have the happy faculty of conforming or adapting yourself to all persons, even to the taking on of the ways and manners of others. You can imitate, do what you see done.

You are also joyous, hopeful, mirthful, playful, and very fond of fun; will not only *enjoy* a joke, but *create* it, and would be quick at *repartee*. You are almost *hilarious* in your nature.

You can measure well by the eye, and judge of sizes, forms, proportions and distances; can keep the centre of gravity in riding, climbing, or marching; would be a correct accountant if accustomed to figures; would be systematic and methodical.

You are fond of music; will enjoy it highly, though you may not compose it. You would be ready as a writer or a speaker, and if trained to it, would excel in composition or in conversation.

You can reason well; comprehend *persons*, as well as *facts* and details; can criticise, compare, elucidate, and make your knowledge available on all occasions; but if you excel in one thing more than in another, it is in your ability to discern the motives of strangers, often at the first interview. You can read them as others read books, and know even at a glance whom to trust and whom not to trust.

This power is intuitive, and introduces you at once to the innermost thoughts and feelings of those whom you meet. It is a sort of psychological impression, and when you heed it, it will guide you correctly.

If you *marry*, select for a companion one who is healthy, intelligent and religiously disposed; one with whom you may be an equal, for you never will consent to play second, nor be held in subjection, but you must have equal rights and privileges in all things. You cannot bear restraint, nor are you inclined to dictate. You simply wish to be free, and to place your accountability between yourself and your Maker, rather than to man.

# CONTENTS

# HIT

# CHAPTER I

# LOVE AND MARRIAGE

There is nothing of greater interest to all classes of people, in all times of life, than Love and Marriage questions—because all people are affected, directly or indirectly, either by their own, by those with whom they are associated in every day relations, or by the ties of consanguinity. And yet there is nothing that society meddles with so much in an unhealthful manner, thus preventing clear and dignified thought and action in a healthy direction.

The affections need cultivating, guarding and guiding. It would be sophistry, to say that anger, malice, revenge, or any of the so-called *unamiable* traits of character, should be allowed to be exercised without reason to restrain them, on the ground of *naturalness*; and yet there is a class of people who *openly*,—and a still larger class who *clandes-*

*tinely*, live out the belief, that if one is pleased with another, the love element of our being should be exercised without restraint; and such a vast number have so little of Love, and so much of excitability of sexuality, that great wrongs are inflicted on soul and body, to an incalculable extent.

The grossest people, those not far removed from the animals, cannot understand that there can be, that it is possible in human nature, for a soul love, unmixed with sensuality; they cannot comprehend the existence of a deeper and purer element than they possess themselves; and yet, if they were to reason upon the subject, they would believe that, as others possess various gifts vastly superior to their own, why not the pure love element?

That some are born with greater musical, mathematical, logical and artistic powers or capabilities than others, no intelligent person will deny; but that cultivation makes all of these more perfect and useful, is equally true. Suppose we apply the same to Love. Observation must teach that the most affectionate and loving, have so cultivated themselves, that they *can* Love without a mixture of what is usually termed animal passion, and unless married people have this kind of cultivation, the time *must* come when they will become weary of each other, and desire nothing so much as to be *anywhere* but at home.

Every faculty of our being is capable of cultivation and of restraint—and our reason and observation are for the purpose of assisting and inducing action in effecting these designs, of correcting the evil, and cultivating the good.

Combativeness and destructiveness, and all the passions of the brain, are all good in their places, and were all designed for a wise purpose, just as much as Love.

The most truly logical on the Love and Marriage question, live the best lives and obtain the most substantial and permanent blessings of earth.

The few, O the lamentably *few*, cases of observation, teach us this truth! But away down in the depths of the soul, where no false reasoning can ever penetrate, we see, we hear, we *feel*, the evidence.

True conjugal companionship is the greatest blessing of which mortals can conceive in this life—to know that there is supreme interest in *one* individual, and that it is reciprocated. Everything sinks into nothingness without such an assurance, for all that earth can give without it, is but as "sounding brass and a tinkling cymbal." Nothing can make an individual more wretched than to lose confidence. It is not simply that which is lost in the *one* person, but the distrust that is felt in all humanity.

The deceived, who has placed implicit trust in one so nearly related as is one conjugally, can not soon and easily (without much evidence) trust those with whom there has been but an ordinary or general acquaintance.

The most beautiful stories of faithfulness; the most charming poems, with heart and soul richness; the sweetest and tenderest songs, seem but a solemn mockery of a once believed-to-be reality.

Love is ever placed upon a pedestal, with pictures of cheating lies and living sepulchres. Try as hard as the poor victim can, to tear all down and trample under the feet of forgetfulness, the "Nevermore" of the "Raven" is intent on drowning every other thought of sound, and every possibility of confidence in mortals.

And then, as if to test the capacity for enduring and suffering, the world heaps its scorn upon the poor subjects, driving them into a far deeper gulf, when, but for such treatment, while struggling so hard to *try* to feel that there was a little Love in the world, souls to society and themselves, might have been saved!

Is any one who has caused such depths of sorrow, capable of Love and fit for marriage? There is no need of a pause for a reply. In every pulsation of your heart, there is an unmistakable *no*?

Tupper has beautifully expressed his ideas on this subject, in the following words:

"Love is an angel mind breathed into a mortal.
Love is the devotion of the heart; in all its grandeur
Is a sordid man capable of Love?
Hath a seducer known it?
Can an adulterer perceive it?
Or he that changeth often, can he feel its purity?"

The polygamists, whether in Utah, Oneida, or scattered about the world generally, under moral or religious canopies, all fail to comprehend the meaning of true affection. But the polygamists and the communists, who openly in their life declare Love and lust to be one and the same, and that they have rights that are inalienable in passional directions, that their respective societies designate, are a thousand fold better than the people outside, who are preaching morality, and practicing the most underhanded and trickish measures, to accomplish the same results under their false colors, not only, but cruelly thrusting others out of society, who are their victims, as soon as they are tired of them, or have made new conquests, or are forced by publicity to take such a step. As men are the makers of general laws, so are they of social laws, and this one they keep *rigidly*, when the victim has been their own.

We have often heard it said, that men always love women, and are their natural protectors, because of their great strength, and great Love. Some men love women as children love dolls, and, as a natural result, treat them just as dolls are cared for. They dress them in all the finery they are able to procure, pet and exhibit them until the clothes become old, and the beautiful color of the face is gone, and the eyes are contracted and dim, and then, like worn out dolls, they are thrown aside for neighbors' dolls, or for some beautiful images in the show windows of false society's market.

In the thousands of such cases, that are all over our country, is it to be wondered at, that a looker into the condition of society as it is, cannot believe that there ever was anything approximating anywhere near genuineness in the affections, between the so-called husbands and wives!

Such cannot sing the soul-satisfying ballad—"Let us grow old together," for they do not desire to do so; like the few who can sing in the spirit, finding beauty and charms in wrinkles, that are entirely wanting in the undeveloped faces of rose and lily colored smoothness.

There is more depth in the old tear-dimmed eye of affection, than in the soul-piercing glance, from the most beautiful and brilliant eyes of youth. Those whose love shall have been constant and faithful, until age shall creep upon them, will assuredly find a calm and peace that shall be in itself true happiness.

The masses will sometime realize that there must be stability in the affections, or there can be no true Love; and if there is no reliability in the affections by having the love concentrated on some one object, a man (as a rule) cannot be fully relied upon, in any of the duties of life, for the fortress of the soul is sooner or later captured by the enemy.

It is well known that a married man, whose affections are properly exercised and directed, succeeds much better in life than the single, unstable lover.

There cannot be love without respect, and there cannot be respect unless there is implicit confidence.

How wretched are two partners in ordinary business relations, when confidence is wanting! But how much more wretched, aye *agonizing*, where it is a life partnership, and confidence and love are both wanting! No jealousies ever creep in, where there is that amount of confidence which should exist between the married, and nothing is more absurd than to say that "the affectionate are always jealous," for it comes from a lack of confidence, instead of an excess of affection.

"Love worketh no evil."

Thousands of women have been accused of being jealous, when they were not so at all, for they were sorrowing over a husband's infidelity. They could not *prove* his vileness, according to the codes of *man*, but it was proved to them, in the severing of the invisible magnetic cable, which can *never* again be so united as to possess its former strength and power.

It is impossible for one unfaithful in the Marriage relation, to come into the presence of the other without feeling a consciousness of that unfaithfulness, and appearing *unworthy* of the confiding one, who trusted all and was deceived.

Law, man-made law, very soon dissolves other partnerships, where there is nothing but *filthy lucre* in the case: but when the heart and soul, and the dearest interests of a *lifetime* are in the question, quibbles are found to chain both soul and body for years and years and *years*, until their effects open an early *grave*, for a body whose soul has been matured, by great and deep wrongs and trials, so that nothing of an earthly nature can hold it any longer.

Many of our States have laws compelling married people to live together, when the wife perfectly loathes the very sight of her husband, and one after another child is given an existence, that is hated by both, before it is born. Each parent sees traits of character in their children, that have been inherited from the other, thus arousing still greater repugnance to their children, (if possible,) and but for public sentiment and law, would as soon deprive them of their unwelcome existence, as they would a viper that comes unasked and undesired into their presence. The children are wretched, having a most unhappy organization, fit for any sort of misdemeanor, or crime. Still, there are people who wonder how such terrible crimes could ever have been committed in a Christian country, as are recorded daily.

There are members of churches, who so read the Bible, as to make out that it is the *duty* of wives to submit to all sorts of oppression, in a Christian manner, while husbands outrage every sense of common *decency*, to say nothing about their *sworn obligations* to love and cherish their wives.

Paul's injunction to obey their husbands is taken to mean the women of to-day, instead of in the lifetime of Paul, when he saw that the men were so corrupt and tyrannical, that in the treatment of their slave-wives they would only be much more abusive if, they did not treat their husbands as the lords they assumed to be. Paul's advice was in quite a different age, and to quite a different people, and was given as *advice*, and not as a *command* of God. It was 170 years after Christ's birth before there was any religious ceremony in marriage.

Untold wrongs to wives are perpetrated all over our land, under cover of a false construction of "the words of the Book of books," which, if rightly understood, would induce all mankind to live out the principles of humanity, but another name for giving to every human being, *rights and liberties* that are fully guaranteed them by their having an existence. Any law or custom that deprives a being of individuality, in any of the relations of life, contravenes the great laws of Deity, thus bringing evil results, as the legitimate consequence.

Men and women should enter into the social contract of marriage, as equal and life-long partners. No young lady, when she is being courted, and flattered, and petted, for a moment supposes that *her* lover *can* ever be so brutal as for a moment to ever wish her to be his slave, and the idea of his assuming the position of *master* or *tyrant*, is to her perfectly preposterous. She feels that, as she is *entitled*, by her intelligence, her purity, nobleness, and worthiness, in every respect, to be treated as an *equal* and *individual* in *all* the relations of life, that she will be treated accordingly. But she can have no guarantee of any better usage than the *law* compels.

O how terribly wretched, beyond comparison, when woman realizes that her purity and affection, and all her worthy traits of character, fail to bring the appreciation she has a *right* to expect! and she too, tied for life to one whose *own* soul was annihilated, the hour he deemed the law gave him the possession of another soul! Too true, *lamentably* true, that there was but one soul in the twain; the one possessing it in reality, and the other possessing it by *law*!

"What God hath joined together, let not man put asunder."

The Bible has no command that is more sacred than this; not even the one *"thou shalt not kill,"* and it matters not how forgiving the injured party may be, the penalty *must* be felt, not only in *this* life, but that which is to come. The soul that sinneth, *must* suffer, and the innocent are brought to suffering through the iniquities of the guilty.

Men, the *protectors* of women, usurp the power to make laws that oppress your mothers and sisters, a thousand-fold worse than human language can express, and then you call it sacred marriage, when it is only legalized villainy!

A woman may see her husband *kill* another person, which may be the work of but a few moments, and law makes her a competent witness against that husband; but she may see him disregard his marriage obligations, any number of times, and her husband can laugh her in the face, with a paramour in her own house, who shall drive her from her own room, and yet *law* says she is not a competent witness against her husband in such a case. She may suffer untold agonies in her pure soul, and yet be compelled to live with him, or be posted, or be called jealous and fault-finding, and exacting, when, if there was a *real* cause for leaving him, why does she not *prove* it?

You call such, *sacred* marriages, and a woman is a *free lover*, or a some terrible creature, if she ever leaves a husband for his infidelity, if she cannot *prove* it, when you have made a law for the purpose of *preventing* her from *proving* his iniquities. He may, under a very smooth face, be one of the *vilest* men living, and his wife suffer a *thousand* agonies, that are a thousand-fold *worse than murder*, and yet your laws let her suffer, while she might be free from the *villain*, if law gave her as much a right to protect her marriage purity, as it does to witness against the crime of murder, which is but a *play of indiscretion*, compared to the *great physical* and *moral wrongs*, that are allowed in the marriage relation, without the power to free herself, under the laws of some of our great States that have so much regard for the *sanctity of marriage*, that it closes nearly every avenue of freedom from the guilty party of the *terribly perverted* institution.

There *can* be nothing more beautiful, than the true marriages that are so rare, in the great mass of the so-called "what God has joined together," when He has had nothing to do with the matter, any more than suffering their consummation and continuance.

But there *can* be a beautiful confidence, where soul reads soul, appreciatingly, and neither tries to deceive the other. Such, and such alone, are truly married, and *must* recognize and practice the great and beautiful laws of true marriage.

It has been said that the "truest men and the truest women, are those who are the most under the influence of each other."

But the usages of society are such, that it is not an easy matter for the truly congenial to understand each other. Many a man has married, who supposed that *he*, above all others in the world, was preferred for a husband, when *nothing* could be farther from the truth.

Were it not impolitic for women to confess this truth, few could be found who would not admit that, if they had been as free to select a husband, as men are to select wives, they would not have married as they did! But women's failure to come to the confessional on this subject, does not prevent every individual of observation from seeing, not only, the ill-assorted marriages on every hand, but the terrible results which crop out in the shape of affinities, communities, desertions, and murders of various kinds, beside a host of evils too numerous to mention.

Society pays a premium to women for being deceitful, by being sure to abuse those who dare to be honest and frank.

A woman does not dare to show the least preference for a man, until *he* has made the first advances, and young men are taught that such a course is *unladylike*, and bold, and to be beautifully feminine and charming, she must carry on a course of gauzy deception, pretending she does not care especially for him, until *he* will seek to win *her* regard, and even *then* she must keep up a *little* deceit.

Men talk about the great intuitive powers of woman, and declare her superior to *them* in this intuition, yet they ridicule the idea of society allowing her to exercise this *intuition* in the selection of a husband. We are far behind the people of *Persia*, for there was a time when the women were authorized by law to select husbands for themselves, if they owned a hut, or a fishing boat.

There should be perfect freedom for woman to select a partner for life in a straight forward, honest and honorable manner.

Queen Victoria has set the world a praiseworthy example, instead of intriguing and deceiving.

Noble men must feel themselves highly honored, when they realize that society is in such a condition that honesty in lifelong interests, is almost unknown. But men themselves are to blame for this condition, for just as long as woman is politically a slave, having no voice in making the laws by which she is governed, and compelled to pay taxes to carry on man's government, she must of necessity do the best she can in her slave chains.

The time is not distant when women as wives, and mothers, and sisters, will be equal with men in all the social, and political relations of life; and then men themselves will be astonished that they *could* have opposed what was really for their *own* interest, as well as that of women. It was many years before men could understand that an intelligent and well educated woman was a better wife and companion than an ignorant one.

Women cannot be deprived of God-given rights, or of Republican rights, without men being sufferers as well as women.

We could not understand how much disadvantage the whites labored under, in consequence of the slavery of the blacks, until the slaves were freed, and the scales, one after another, fell from our eyes.

The oppressor is of necessity a tyrant, and the oppressed are always slaves, and *as* slaves they feel that *slavery* is not the natural condition of one human being, and if there is not a revolt, sooner or later, there is a constant study to gain advantage by the *science* of deception.

Slave deceives master, and master deceives slave. So is the marriage relation in thousands of instances. The fault is in the *perversion* of the institution, and not the institution itself. And men and women are both required to make laws, which shall be just to both, and not in the least oppressive to either, before the generality of marriages will be the beautiful companionship that our Heavenly Father intended.

That there are but few nations that are in a degree just to women in their courting and marriage relations the following will show.

There is no criterion by which one can judge so correctly in regard to the broad, liberal and just ideas of the people of a state, or a country, as by a knowledge of their Marriage customs, and *vice versa.*

The facts that are contained in this part of the chapter, have been gathered from different sources, for the purpose of contrasting them with the social and national laws in the various States of our Union, and as they were gleaned for that purpose *alone*, the author neglected to note the different sources from which they were obtained. The greater part of the same were found in extracts from letters of travellers, who witnessed such customs, and it would be impossible to give the credit to the sources due. Those from various books, in libraries and elsewhere, were noted down for the same purpose as just stated, and in most instances without attempting to remember the writer's name.

The reader will observe that in some countries, Marriage is positively a religious rite, while in others, their religion has nothing to do with the matter, but in *many*, that it is a combination of legal and religious ceremonies, and in still others, of neither.

In the United States, the laws are so various in the different States, and among different religious sects, that our country represents not only a few beauties, but many absurdities. In some States, a couple cannot marry without a license, but a justice of the peace can join their hands and ask them if they will live as husband and wife, and when they respond "yes," he pronounces them such, and it is legal. In other States, New York, for instance, a Marriage is perfectly legal, with the ceremony just stated, *without* any license, it matters not what time of day or night a couple call for such ceremony. Indeed, it is still easier, for a simple declaring in presence of witnesses, that they will live together as husband and wife, at any hour of day or night, renders the marriage lawful, and it cannot be annulled, except for *crim. con.* (adultery).

The Jews in our country live up to their ideas of not committing the sin of marrying a Gentile; they control their own Marriages in their churches, and acknowledge no power out of the church to grant divorces, unless they divorce the couple *first* in the church of their own faith.

Roman Catholics must be married by a priest of their own church, and a divorce is never granted under any circumstances.

In the State of Kentucky, a Marriage is not legal unless a license is procured, not only, but a man at hand who will go bail in the sum of $200, that both are fit persons to marry, no matter what their ages are, even if they are heads of families.

A marriage is legal in some States, if the girl is but

twelve years old, and the boy fourteen, while in others, the woman must be eighteen, and the man twenty-one. But such *children Marriages* will not be suffered, when women are enfranchised, and have a voice in the making of the laws. Congress ought to make general Marriage laws, and no State ought to have the power to legislate in matters of the most vital interest to the people of every State. Frauds and deceptions of every grade are constantly perpetrated, resulting from the different Marriage laws of the various States, and although women and children are great sufferers, still men are occasionally victimized.

Only a few of the Absurdities that might be mentioned in our dear native land, have been presented to the public, in the light that they really deserve; but enough has been said to prevent so much boasting about "our institutions being superior to those of all the rest of the world," when they are far from being simply *just*, and are in reality, in some respects, greatly inferior to some of those of other countries.

No pretension is made to give the reader *all* the Beauties and Absurdities of the Marriage relation all over the world, but only such as are, in the modest estimation of the writer, some of the most prominent ones.

The Quakers marry themselves, with their promises to each other to live as husband and wife while life lasts. This is usually in their own churches, but sometimes at the bride's house, before a number of witnesses, who sign the marriage certificate or contract.

In England, when a marriage engagement is made, the

couple, and all their friends, are not only free to speak of it, but they consider it a duty which they owe society, that an honorable engagement may be known, in order to prevent any others from placing their affections on the affianced. It often occurs that they are engaged several years, and if they finally conclude to break their engagement they are free to state the fact without seeking to injure each other. They do not sit up late at night, but they visit in the drawing-room in the presence of the family, or at least the mother. Few who are engaged, ever go to any place without a third person, and no couple could be in public alone, without people supposing that they were engaged to be married.

A Marriage must be solemnized before twelve at noon, to make it legal. The ceremony is usually performed in church. When they start upon their bridal tour they throw an old slipper of the bride out of the carriage. The bride submits to the tyrannical custom of promising to "honor and obey."

England is not the only country that would do well to import the Marriage ceremony from Sicily, where they promise to "Love and cherish" each other. Neither is it the only country that still has the barbarous law, that if a wife flees from her husband, he can have her arrested and *compel* her to live with him! In the time of George the Third, about the year 1772, an act was passed in Parliament to prevent all Marriages of the princes over twenty-five years of age without the approval of that body, and another to prevent princes marrying under twenty-five without the consent of the King. Without the consent of the authorities just mentioned, the Marriages were pronounced null and void.

A woman's name is as dear to her as a man's is to him, and custom ought, and will prevail, where each will keep their own names when they marry, and allow the children at a certain age to decide which name they will prefer. It would make no more confusion in families than where a man's widowed sister is keeping house for him with her own and his children together, or where a widow with children marries a widower with children. That some women are well satisfied to have their identity perfectly swallowed up in Marriage by losing both surnames and Christian names, when they have been guilty of no crimes, to make it desirable to hide them, is indeed wonderful.

Miss Jane Jones is lost in Mrs. John Smith. Who would dream that she is the same person she was an hour since? A woman must be called *Mrs.* to let all the world know she is married, and if there is a necessity for this, why not call a man *Misterer* for the purpose of enlightening the world as to his condition?

Let men and women stand as equals. We believe in *men's* rights as well as women's, and if there are any advantages to be gained by the titles of Marriage, let men share them as well as women.

In France, if a gentleman asks a lady to dance with him more than once at a social party, he is considered to be in love with her. An unmarried gentleman does not sit near an unmarried lady, in company, but as soon as he seats her after having danced, he takes a chair near another gentleman or a married lady, although the couple are attentive to each other while dancing. The marriages are in the Roman Catholic faith, and the husband takes the wife's name if she desires him to do so. There must be four witnesses to a Marriage ceremony, and there must be two distinct ceremonies, one of state and one of the church.

In the interior of Africa, Dr. Livingstone found that in the marriage relation the man took the name of the woman, and was bound to go and reside in the native village with the wife, if she chose to have him. He is bound to provide her mother with firewood for life. If the Marriage is not a pleasant one, the woman alone can have a divorce, and the children belong to her.

The men have several wives, but the first one is the one by whose name the husband is called.

The wives allow polygamy, as the husbands are on such a low plane, that it would be useless to attempt to prevent it, although they have an equal voice in making the laws. The men ask their wives before engaging in any occupation or job of labor.

On a small island near Mull and Iona, on the northwest coast of Scotland, a race of people live, who subsist mostly on fish, wild birds' eggs, and oat meal. The marriage portion of a bride is an iron kettle, and a long rope. The latter is made on the island, and used for the purpose of swinging under the shelving rocks, and securing the birds and fowls' eggs. The young men are said to marry for the sake of being supported.

The marriage of people belonging to the Brahmin

class, living in Calcutta, is very complicated, and occupies five days.

The first day is devoted to washing the bridegroom and bride in the sacred waters of the Ganges, and to various ceremonies intended to guard them against the influences of the *evil eye*. The second day the two fathers join their children's hands, and pour over them seven measures of water, seven of corn, and seven of milk, while the officiating Brahmin reads the portion of the law which treats of conjugal life and its duties. A cord is then put round the bridegroom's shoulder and a great ring, typical of marriage, is fastened to the neck of the bride.

On the third day, the bride and bridegroom march seven times round the sacred fire. On the fourth day, they dine together in public. On the fifth day, an offering of rice is sacrificed, the only *religious* ceremony except *suttee*, to which a woman is admitted. The ceremonies terminate by a triumphal procession.

In Sicily, marriages are according to the rites of the Greek Church. The bride is richly dressed in the ancient costume of gold and silver brocade, ornamented with precious stones. She walks to church with the bridegroom, leaning on his arm, while just before them, a number of musicians walk leisurely along, enlivening the occasion with music. A boy in a long white robe accompanies the wedding party, carrying on his head a basket containing two nuptial crowns, and two wedding rings, one of gold and the other of silver.

At the moment the Priest gives the gold ring to the

man, and the silver one to the woman, the crowns are placed on their heads, and they promise to love and cherish one another all their lives. The Priest then blesses a goblet of wine, and the bride and bridegroom both drink from the same glass, and divide a morsel of bread. The Priest lays his hands upon their heads and pronounces the blessings of the church upon them. The veil which hides them from the gaze of the spectators is withdrawn, and the ceremony closes with a grave dance in the church, the music being from the organ and orchestra. The Priest and his clerk take part in the dance.

In Prussia, the minister *gives* his services in marrying people, and makes the bride a present.

In the good old times, a Persian girl who owned a little property—a hut or fishing boat—was thereby authorized to select a husband herself. If she wished to commence her search for a husband, she hung up her blue apron in front of the door of the house, and posted herself behind it. The young men of the village passed by the apron one by one in a long procession, dressed in their best Sunday clothes. As soon as the right one appeared, the girl rushed out, threw her arms around his neck, and within three weeks there was a wedding.

In Syria, a few years since, 3,000 Christian girls were carried off to Turkey, and sold as wives, the sale being the only marriage ceremony.

The ceremony of marriage in Java is very curious. The bride and bridegroom are brought before the Dukum or Priest, in the house they are to inhabit. They make an obeisance towards the south, then to the hearth, or fire-place, which is to be the scene of their domestic bliss. The third obeisance is towards the earth. Next, they raise their eyes to the upper story of the house for a few moments, after which the Priest says a long prayer, asking for a blessing on both husband and wife. The wife then goes through a ceremony indicative of her humility and will-ingness to serve her husband in all things, by washing his feet in public; after which the friends make them presents of household implements, in return for which they offer their friends betel nuts.

Among a tribe of people called Kocch, that live on the hills in India, as soon as a couple are married, the bride-groom goes to live with the family of the bride, and all his property is made over to her. In the island of Celebes, men were allowed to marry as many wives as they could sup-port, just as they are in Utah, under Brigham Young.

In Hungary, they do not marry very young. The gen-tleman pays marked attention to the lady for three, four, and sometimes five years. The gentleman employs an agent to exchange rings with the lady, and ask her hand. The lady's father, in the presence of several witnesses, gives his consent. On the wedding morning, the young man's friends repair with joyous shouts, to the house of the bride's father, for the purpose of carrying off the bride, whom they conduct to church with the bridegroom.

After the ceremonies at church, the pair are escorted to the bride's home, amid firing of pistols, guns, and all the vil-lage artillery. The nuptial house is generally found closed, and stones are hurled at the door. When the door is opened, a table is seen, sumptuously covered with viands. The heroes of the occasion are seated with their intimate friends, and the whole company observe deep silence, while the blessing is asked. The proceedings terminate with a dancing party.

On the Sunday morning preceding a marriage in Bretague, every invited guest sends a present to the young couple. On the bridal day, a band of music leads in a procession of friends who repair to the bride's house, where the door is immediately opened by a man with a wand in his hand, who points out to the party, in a long rhymed speech, that there is a castle *somewhere* in the neighborhood, where so gallant a company cannot fail to be well entertained. The bridegroom has also brought his poet, who gives verse for verse, and compliment for compliment.

When the company demand the bride, the wrong person is brought forward. First an old woman, then a child, then a widow, and afterwards one of the bridesmaids. When this sport has continued until the patience of the company is exhausted and the bridegroom's poet's poetry, the *real* bride is brought forth to greet her betrothed, amidst the shouts of happiness that are heard from the party.

In Ireland, at the fair of Galway, it is a custom for all the marriageable girls to assemble and to tempt all wanting wives, by their captivating charms, to be made more happy for life. Says an American gentleman of the highest character, who was an eye witness, and invited by a nobleman to go and see these girls:—"At twelve o'clock precisely, we went, as directed, to a part of the ground higher than the rest of the field, where we found from sixty to a hundred young women, well-dressed, with good looks and good manners, and presenting a spectacle quite worthy any civil man looking at, and in which I can assure my readers there was nothing to offend any civil or modest man's feelings. There were the marriageable girls of the country, who had come to show themselves, on the occasion, to the young men and others who wanted wives; and this was the plain and simple custom of the fair. I can plainly say that I saw in the custom no very great impropriety—it certainly did not imply that, though they were ready to be had, anybody could have them. It was not a Circassian slave market, where the richest purchaser could make his selection. They were, in no sense of the term, on sale; nor did they abandon their right of choice; but that which is done constantly in more refined society, under various covers and pretences—at theatres, at balls and public exhibitions, I will say nothing of churches—was done by these humble and unpretending people in this straightforward manner."

The Marriage ceremony in Turkey is as follows—A man sends his negro Eunuch to compel a woman he fancies to come to him—after an examination by the future husband, she is turned into his harlem if she suits him. A man is allowed seven wives in one house, and can have as many times seven as he has houses in different towns. When he becomes tired of a wife she is turned out to go her way. The Eunuch is master over these unfortunate women, acting like a shepherd dog, keeping them herded together, and not allowing any one but the Turk to see them.

These women have no education, and are not required to do any work. The one that can master the rest is the favorite with the Turk. It is lawful for him to kill a wife if she violates his rules.

In Russia, the marriageable women are put in market once a year, and the men walk about and view them, and when one is seen that is fancied, a card is put into her hand—she hands hers to the admirer, and the courtship commences.

In Greece, a man will not marry so long as he has a marriageable sister. The youngest son believes it his first duty to see his sisters all provided with husbands.

In some parts of South America, many do not marry until they have raised families. They can marry and have their children baptized, and they inherit the property. But if this is neglected, the property all goes to the church, and the family is left destitute.

Among the Nestorians, on the wedding night, the bridegroom gave the bride a kick with his foot and commanded her to pull off her shoes as a token of her submission.

It has been stated by Plutarch that the Spartans always carried off their brides by a feigned force, in order to make it a legal Marriage. A Spartan woman appeared in public until she was married, but ever after she wore a veil.

In ancient Assyria all the marriageable young girls were sold in a public place at auction, and all the women were provided with husbands. Those who were very handsome sold for large sums, and the money was divided among the plain-looking ones.

A tribe of people in Barbary called Nasamones used to marry by drinking out of each other's hands. The parents arranged the match, and the bride's face was unveiled by the husband for the first time on their wedding day.

It has been stated that in some country the young lady rides a fleet horse, and if she desires to marry, she allows herself to be overtaken, but if the wrong suitor is likely to overtake her, she drops a golden apple, and while he is picking it up, the one she wishes to marry is allowed to overtake her.

Hon. I. S. Diehl, the celebrated Lecturer on Oriental and Bible Lands, relates many curious customs, among which are the two following:

In Armenia the young woman is brought to the mother of her affianced, who, in an angry manner, throws her a bundle of infant's clothes, places a little one in her arms and watches the Miss, who nervously dresses the babe, and if to the satisfaction of the future mother-in-law, she is allowed to marry, but if not, she is sent home to take fresh lessons in the art of babydressing.

In some places, the Circassian women are taken to a market and sold as wives to the highest bidder. Among the Circassians, a young woman is put on a horse's back, and compelled to ride over the plains until caught by some man, the catching being the only Marriage ceremony. It sometimes occurs that the husband is a speculator, and as soon as she is caught, he sends his *property* on another equestrian tour, and sells her to the successful capturer.

In some of the German states, a young woman lives

with her affianced mother a year before her marriage, that she may learn all about household matters.

In Persia, the business of the bridegroom is transacted by an agent, and the contract is one of barter. The wedding festivities at the bride's house last for ten days. On the last day the bridegroom sends the bride her *trousseau*, which consists of rich jewels, dresses and sometimes slaves and attendants. All sorts of wealth is displayed, and sometimes a great pretension is made, by carrying empty boxes. The bride is brought to the husband's house mounted on a camel, or a horse.

The Marriage itself is entirely an affair of bargain and sale, as the bride is taken in consideration of a certain dowry. Now and then the husband objects at the last moment to ratify the engagement he has made, and when his bride is brought home to him, refuses to receive her, stating himself unable or unwilling to pay so much. Then follows a long scene of *bargaining*, always, however, ending in a compromise, for it would be a great disgrace to the bride to be sent back. The marriage is seldom intended to last the lifetime of either party.

Marriages in Norway are usually solemnized in winter, when the peasants are comparatively unoccupied. A week before the ceremony is to take place, messengers are sent around to invite the proprietors and servants of neighboring farms. The room in which the ceremony is to take place, is decorated with green boughs.

After a substantial breakfast, the betrothed couple are brought forward by their relatives, and seated in state in the great room, where the priest blesses them, and when the prayers are finished, proceeds to a table, on which is placed a large plate. Addressing the company generally, he recommends the couple to their notice. The relatives then come forward, and deposit bright new crown pieces in the plate; then come the rich neighbors, who contribute according to their means, and lastly, the poorer friends, who each throw in their mite, towards setting up the household of the new-made wife. The festivities are kept up for two or three days.

In Arabia Felix, the wives were all in common. When a man entered a house, he left his staff at the door as a sign that the woman was engaged.

In Persia, they formerly believed that married people were happier after death than single ones, and so if a person died single, they would marry some one to the corpse before burial. Some people hired persons to be espoused to their relatives who had died single and were buried without having been married.

In India, on the Malabar coast, among some of the lower classes, a man can have but *one* wife, while a woman may have three husbands. All three contribute to the support of the children.

In the mountains of Jamaica, among the Maroons, when a girl is old enough to marry, her parents make a feast, and if a young man agrees with the girl to live together, they are considered married.

In Silesia, the peasants celebrate their Marriages very pompously. The bridal procession is headed by musicians, and the wedding cortege and horses are gaily decked with ribbons. On the Marriage morning, the bridegroom presents himself at the house of the bride, and, after an infinity of prayers, refusals, and cajoleries, the bride is brought forth. She is condemned to listen to a long list of rules for her future conduct and carriage. Then she gives her hand to her betrothed, and he lifts her into the carriage. As they proceed to the church, the guests eat cold provisions, and drink brandy.

After the ceremony at church, the party proceed to the bride's house, where, for three days, they have dancing. Their guests are given roast meat, cakes, beer, and spirits. After the three days have passed, the bride departs in her husband's wagon, often seated on the top of a pile of furniture, which is her dowry. The first person who meets her in her new home, gives her a piece of bread.

When the Egyptian bride leaves her parents' home, for the dwelling of her husband, all her female friends and relatives accompany her, veiled like herself, and march under a *dais*, preceded by musicians and tumblers. The tumblers walk just before the ladies, and go through with various gymnastics, some of which consist in their standing upon their heads. After a sort of triumphal progress, the procession stops at the house of the future husband. Here the visitors are received, and the bride is conducted to the nuptial hall, where the husband, who has never seen his bride's face, though the marriage ceremony is over, is waiting to receive her.

The husband then advances, and lifts the veil that has

hitherto hidden the features of the bride, and so perfect a command have the Mussulmans, in general, that they seldom betray any sign of pleasure or dissatisfaction at the beauty or plainness of the ladies upon whom their choice has fallen. The only male spectators of this ceremony are the brothers and father of the bride, for in Egypt the women are so jealously guarded, that no men are allowed to look at them from their infancy, except their nearest relatives.

In Siberia, the bride is required, on her arrival at her husband's home, to invite guests to a dinner prepared by herself, and if pronounced *good*, it is a recommendation which is above all things to be desired by a woman.

In Japan, the bride's teeth are made black by some corrosive liquid to show that she is married. The laws allow men to marry all relatives except sisters.

In India, the Hindoo widows are not allowed to marry, however young they may be. The very day a girl becomes a widow, her colored clothes, silver and golden ornaments are all taken off. Henceforth, she has to dress in white, and wear no ornaments of any kind whatever during her lifetime. Her daily meals are reduced to one, and that is prepared in the simplest way possible. She is strictly prohibited the use of any sort of animal food. Each widow is required to cook her own food, and to abstain entirely from food and drink two days in every month. On the fast days, when the burning sun dries up the ponds and scorches the leaves of the trees, these poor victims faint and pant in hunger and thirst. If they are dying on the *aku thusty* day, a little water will be put on the lips merely to wet them. They have no hope of ever changing their widowhood in the world.

A recent change in the law, however, now allows the marriage of widows, and a learned Brahmin, the Principal of Calcutta Sanscrit College, is earnestly engaged in redeeming their condition, by introducing the system of widow marriage.

Among some tribes of the North American Indians, the suitor enters the wigwam of the squaw he wishes to marry, and proceeding to the farthest corner of the room, commences throwing a few kernels of corn at the object of his affections, and if she retreats to another corner, and returns the throwing, his addresses are acceptable, but if she leaves the wigwam, he returns to his own. In another tribe, living near civilization, the lover leaves a violin near the door, and if it is taken in by the squaw, he returns and entertains her with music.

We come lastly to the happy bride in New South Wales, *where no clothes are worn*. The Marriage customs in this place are as brutal and savage as the people can well make them. A man, desirous of adding a *gin* or wife, to his establishment assembles a certain number of his particular friends, with whom he sallies forth to dog the footsteps of some neighboring tribe. With admirable patience the marauders watch for a favorable opportunity. When at length one arrives, they throw themselves upon the family, whose alliance their chief is anxious to secure, put all its members to flight, excepting the bride, whom they seize and hold fast.

Frantic with fear, she struggles and yells, but her cries are silenced by blows with a heavy club, and faint and bruised, with her flesh on her back torn, and the blood covering the wounds, she is dragged through the bush. Her husband is the master of his slave and wife, *all in one*, and she is compelled to do all the disagreeable work, and the slightest dereliction of duty is visited by a severe administration of *club law*, from *"her protector."*

# CHAPTER II

# DRESS REFORM

That the style and cut of the covering of the "mortal coil" has had its influence in the marriage relation, from the days of our first parents until now, no one will deny. That the Dress of women has *ever* been just what it should be, in order to protect the person, and allow freedom of motion and circulation, and not make the wearer a slave to it, was not approximated, until some of the Women Physicians of America took the subject in hand, and directed its arrangement in accordance with the laws of health, and the necessities of life. It is a well known fact, that the opposition brought to bear, is in proportion to the importance of the subject to humanity. And hence as Dress Reform for women is of paramount importance, it can be readily seen that the ignoble have ample reasons for opposing what will throw barriers in their path—what will remove the easy facilities for monster vices.

Everything that makes woman in any degree independent of man, and, as a consequence, independent of marriage for support, is frowned down by a certain class of individuals. But when it makes them independent *in* marriage, their opposition is unbounded, and they really seem to feel that they are doing "God service" by persecuting those who are trying to save their physical, and by saving the physical, improving the mental strength.

Strange it is, that men do not understand how much better it would be for *them*, in many respects, if women were all dressed in a hygienic manner; but as they are *not*, they actually do all in their power by tongue and pen, to oppress those who dare to dress hygienically.

There is no doubt that the ignorance of the real principles, and the crude and incorrect ideas of many, induce some people to pursue the course just indicated. But time's surgical instruments will remove the scales from the *Saul's eyes*, and they will be as zealous in *sustaining*, as they are in persecuting.

To elucidate the effects of fashionable Dress upon the marriage relation, we need only say, that, as far as the expensiveness is concerned, that many men will not marry, because the voluminous and numerous Dresses, with their other paraphernalia, requires a small fortune to replenish the ever changing fashionable styles.

Young men are often heard to say that "if a wife's clothes did not cost any more than their own, they could *afford* to marry." It is but natural that honest young men should be *afraid* to marry, when they see their friends so embarrassed in consequence of the extravagance of their wives in Dress. The lessons inculcated by failures in business as a consequence of having a fashionable wife, are learned and pondered over, until the youthful affections have waned, and the years of adaptation have passed.

It is not only *silly* that an immortal mind should be absorbed for half a lifetime, on fashionable follies, to be arranged on the "casket" that contains this invisible piece of immortality, but it is a *sinful waste of time and energies*; both of which are essential in many directions that are at present overlooked. The thousand perplexities of fashionable Dress, wear so upon the temper of a woman, that she cannot be amiable. A new garment is scarcely finished before a later fashion has made its appearance, and something *new*, or an alteration in the *old*, suggests itself, and the devotee of fashion, if she is *poor*, is nervous over the expense and labor, that are unending; if she is *rich*, over the stupidity of dressmakers, and their slowness in finishing their work, even with the sewing machine to hasten the finishing of dozens of tucks and puffs and ruffles!

So much of the nervous energy is expended on Dress, and dressing, and carrying the burdensome stuff, that a morbid sensibility is induced which women cannot prevent. At the exhibition of this, men lose their patience, believing there is no necessity for a woman ever to be so nervous and easily annoyed at little matters. Not only does the husband and father suffer from this continuous irritability, but the children that *are* and those that *are to be*, partake of the same.

It is time that parents *felt* the responsibility that rests upon them, in regard to the transmission of highly wrought susceptible organizations to their children, that make them so *wretchedly sensitive* to all sorts of earth-life influences.

Let a horse be compelled to wear a harness that is uncomfortable, and with all his great strength of nerves, but a little time will elapse before he is so restless that his driver feels obliged to seek out and remedy the irritating cause. But if a human being writhes under something that injures the nervous system, others are not as careful as they should be, to ascertain the *cause*, and hence the censure under which many poor wives labor.

The effects of Dress upon *woman's physical being specially* are such as to injure the happiness of the marriage relation. Few young women are to be found, that are fit for marriage, because they have been dressed in such a manner that weakness if not mechanical displacements have resulted.

Scarcely a woman can be found old enough to marry, who is not afflicted with some ailment produced by wearing an unhygienic Dress. From the crown of the head to the soles of the feet, the women are unhealthfully attired, and as there can be no happiness without health, it is obvious that the marriage relation as well as every social relation is embittered when there is no necessity for the same, unless there be a necessity for pleasing a vitiated taste, to the exclusion of health.

Nearly every roof covers a debilitated woman. No one will, for a moment, harbor the idea that God intended such a condition. Even half civilized or savage life is better in some respects than those professed-to-be highest enlightened conditions of society. To illustrate: In China the women compress the feet, but they allow freedom of the chest. In India they wear heavy anklets, but they do not wear long or heavy skirts, injuring women *as* women, and posterity also. In Kamschatka they do not tie up their hair, and put weights of false hair on their heads, crazing them with pain or benumbing the whole cranial surface.

In Turkey, the fact is recognized, that the women's limbs are flesh and blood as well as the men's, and are therefore susceptible to the influences of the weather, and need to be as well protected; and hence the custom of the sexes dressing nearly alike. Those who would find fault with the men of that country, for *allowing* the women to dress like them, (instead of wearing our most fashionable clothes, or rather those of Paris,) would immediately be credited with weak or bad motives.

As women are distinct, separate individuals, *in* the marriage relation as well as *out* of it—as they are sharers of the great labors, and the greater sorrows and burdens of life, there are as *great* or *greater* reasons, why they should be as hygienically dressed as men; and their minds and hearts and consciences, are capable, and will direct them right, just as soon as the way is opened and woman has sweet *liberty* to live up to her noble womanhood, without being hampered and cramped in this direction.

The credentials of the consciousness of the stinted growth of the mental interior, are visible in the faces of the women who are carrying the terrible burdens of Dress, that *does* result in so much of real unhappiness in the marriage relation. A husband has no more right to dictate about the cut of his wife's clothes, than has the wife to interfere with her husband's, and it is time that the barbarous ideas of men assuming such prerogatives, were swept away, and the inherent *right* of woman to dress as she pleases established.

God has either given noble capacities to woman, or He has given her power to receive them, for the fact is evident that she is in *possession* of them, and has a firm disposition to appropriate the same, even if against the express wishes of men; believing as she does that powers for good were not created to moulder unexercised.

Thousands of the wrongs to woman, would be prevented, if women dressed in a hygienic manner, and those wrongs that are not at all to be legislated upon, because they are beyond the sphere of human legislatures. One of the great sources of unhappiness in the marriage relation, results directly from the chilling influences that freeze up the sympathies of wives, that have been so overburdened with their clothes, that they could not cultivate the flowers of beauty in the garden of the soul, where the chilling winds of nervousness were constantly blowing away all beautiful sentiments.

If men were *really* what they *profess* to be, "the protectors of women," they would never arrest one for dressing herself in a comfortable and health and life saving manner. They would not attempt to compel women to dress so that the facilities for vice would always be easy, but would sanction a Dress that is quite the reverse, and no man would attempt to invade the family circle of his neighbor. But *until* the "good time coming" comes, when women can dress hygienically without being *martyrized*, thousands of wrongs and sorrows must result every year, that are perfectly needless, aye, *agonizing!*

The idea that "women cannot be distinguished from men," is a piece of *bosh* that was remedied according to the ideas of the men in the latter part of the fourteenth century, by compelling the women to always carry a *distaff* in one hand, so that there should be no mistake in regard to the sex.

A vast amount of the many troubles of married life, results because of the *illness of wives who are debilitated by Dress*. So alarmingly great has this "general debility" become, that there is not a thoroughly educated M.D. to be found, who does not know that there is scarcely a woman who is not a sufferer from the wearing of long Dresses, even if they fall but to the ankles. There is a weight and swaying motion that nothing can overcome. There is an excess of clothing on some portions of the system, and a deficiency on others. No women are dressed in such a manner that the warmth is equally distributed, except the *Dress Reformers*, and such alone are attired in a manner that will not produce or aggravate mechanical displacements of the abdominal and pelvic viscera.

The greatest sorrows from which women suffer to-day, are those physical, moral, and mental ones, that are caused by their unhygienic manner of dressing! The want of the *ballot* is but a *toy* in comparison! But time and a seeming propriety, prevent the author from making full elucidations and comparisons in this book, as it is for the *general* reader, and is not for women exclusively.

The wretched manner in which little children are dressed before they have a personal control of their clothes, is figured up by sextons to the tune of many thousands every year. In 1860, 300,000 deaths occurred before the age of five years! In the same year, 77,309 deaths resulted from consumption, and inflammation of the lungs!

Has Dress nothing to do with the happiness of the marriage relation, when the parting of friends, who *died of dress* or the improper arrangement of Dress, fills the soul with an amount of sorrow that is almost insupportable?

There *are* those who seem to care very little about *life*, only as it serves them to display a beautiful face, and thus with open eyes to the suicidal manner in which they dress, continue to violate hygienic laws, and very soon *destroy* what Aristotle called "one of the most precious gifts of nature;" what Theophrastus called "a mute eloquence;" what Diogenes called "the most forcible letter of recommendation;" what Plato called "the privilege of nature;" what Bion called "a good that does not belong to the possessor, because it is impossible to give one's self beauty."

It is however possible to *preserve* beauty, even after the frosts of age shall have appeared, if one shall have dressed in a hygienic manner, and also to preserve an *increasing beauty of mind*, that must always be an accompaniment of one who is in good health and aspiring after what is better and nobler than the fashionable follies of Dress, that covers all sorts of evils, and creates thousands of sorrows in the home circles.

Let our clergymen of *all creeds*, imitate the Pope of Rome, and come out boldly, and talk in fitting language against the evils of so much Dress. His Holiness concluded a long letter as follows, in exhorting women to "cultivate their minds; cultivate their hearts; cultivate virtue; for all of glory cometh from within," and not from Dress.

Again we assert that, *from the crown of the head to the soles of the feet*, women are dressed in an unhygienic manner, while men assume all the comforts and conveniences of Dress that they desire, without any one saying unto them, why do ye thus? We may, in our Christian enlightenment, talk of the absurdity of the Chinese pinching and deforming women's feet, but if we had a particle of real modesty we would never mention it in the face of the facts of outrages a thousand-fold worse.

It is stated that the most fashionable American belles have submitted to the removing of the little toe on each foot, for the purpose of being able to wear a very small shoe. It is a fact that all of the vital organs of women are so compressed by stays or corsets that health is impaired and life shortened, not only, but the lives of their children are monstrous disappointments as it regards length, and in all other respects. Woman's "make up" generally after having been given from her mother a feeble constitution, is one mass of everchanging absurdities.

## THE HEAD

There is no way the hair can be worn without injury, save in a perfectly free and flowing manner, except it be to plait the same, and let it fall without being a weight or burden on the head. There are numerous cases of those in comparative health who cannot endure even the latter mode; indeed they cannot endure the weight of the hair, if it fall longer than men's usually does. Astonishing as it may seem, the weight causes an intense pain, as though a heavy weight was attached to the hair.

Coarsely organized women cannot understand this, any more than men, but such women do very well understand what a relief it is to be freed from chignon, extra braids, frizzes, curls, rats, mice, combs, pins, etc. etc., and they almost without exception complain of pains in the head, which result from the wearing of these extras, and the compression caused by tying of the hair, and the strings and elastics to keep the same arranged.

Many an O dear! escapes the lips of women, who, before going out, must perform the head gearing labors, that they declare are so tiresome. The first thought is the arranging of the hair, and the constant thought afterward, is to be careful not to get it disarranged; and the head must be held just so, and there is a constant feeling of being all fixed up, which one cannot get out of their brains, as long as the fixings are painfully reminding them of their presence.

Who can reasonably expect that a woman can be of an amiable disposition who is undergoing a species of torture, at the very citadel of where dispositions are manufactured? Who can reasonably expect that the mother will be able to give everything that is desirable to her children in nature, when she is herself having the mental quality producer in torture all the waking moments of the months that she is giving being, life, soul, to a little immortality?

Dress up the heads of lady Floras, lady Greys, lady Temples, or any other of the great horse raisers; let them be in absolute discomfort all through their lives from the same tortures that the mothers of human beings wear on their heads, and we would soon see the results in their ladyships' colts, in their dispositions and intelligence. Of what use or value is a magnificently formed horse that is wanting in intelligence, and with a balky disposition? The balky traits are the mental ones that are inherited, and generally from the mother.

The mass of men have long since learned how to treat the animal, and it is to be hoped that in the course of a dozen or twenty centuries more they will learn that the happiness of the marriage relations of their children depends upon principles not far remote from those already learned in the animal kingdom.

## THE BODY

1. The first great principle in the clothing of the body is, that there shall be perfect freedom of motion.

2. The second, that there should be an equal distribution of the clothing.

3. The third, that the arrangement should be such that as little of vitality should be expended in carrying it about, as is possible.

There are no women in the world who live these three principles, except those who wear the American Reform Dress in its perfect condition, as we shall describe on another page. It will be readily seen, from the facts we bring, that no woman can wear the ordinary long dress, falling to the ankles, and live the principles we here set forth; for arrange it as best one can, all of the above principles are but partially carried out.

## FREEDOM OF MOTION

In the first place, there cannot be perfect freedom of motion, when the dress reaches to the ankles, as there is a resistance to overcome at every step, as a feeble woman always feels most sensitively. If hoops are worn, there is the atmospheric pressure to overcome to a great extent in front, when walking against the wind, and the same to *resist* when walking from the same. If hoops are not worn, then the same result, with the annoyance of the clothes hitting against the ankles and legs, and often being caught between the ankles and knees. To train oneself in such a manner that the ordinary resistance may be in a measure overcome, produces that extra swing, or those extra motions of the body that are called "womanly," but which would soon be manly enough, if men carried the burdens of dress in the same way that women do.

Take the strongest horse, and put bands just in front of his back legs, and see if he would not make the same uncomfortable movements. If *sex* had anything to do with the extra moves of the body in walking, why do we not see it in the horses? or why do we hear so much about women wearing Reform Dresses, walking so much like men? (if they had not worn the ordinary Dress until the terrible habits were almost unalterable).

One cannot labor and suffer in a freedom-of-motion-obstructed Dress for years, without becoming fixed in habits of motion that such obstruction produces as a natural consequence, and the very grace of a trailing Dress, that we hear lauded so much, and for which so much of life is sacrificed, is produced by the extra painful moves of a tortured body. The same moves in a Reform Dress would be as ridiculous as they would be in a man. Taste is vitiated, and the great laws of easy and healthy reproduction are ignored when such absurdities are practiced by women, and lauded by men.

There is not perfect freedom of motion of any part of the body. The arm sizes are either so small that the arms cannot be reached above the head, or in any direction without wearying them, or they are cut so far off the shoulders and down on the arms, that the same result is produced, and the great mass of women cannot arrange their hair without resting their arms many times, for in spite of *will*, they fall powerless by their sides, because of the compression where the waist ends, and the sleeve begins. The waist being tight also, or at least a snug fit, is one cause of the tired sensation of the arms.

The snug fit of the waist of the Dress or corsets, prevents freedom of motion, of respiration, digestion, assimilative circulation of the blood, and of the nervo-vital fluid. It prevents the freedom of the muscles of the lower part of the chest, and the upper part of the legs; producing a weariness of the bony structure, both at their origin and insertion.

When there is perfect freedom of Dress, there is in respiration, a gentle motion of even these muscles, as well as of the intercostal and abdominal muscles. But the great mass of women have so paralyzed them, that one not well versed in the science of the human system, would scarcely believe, that, from their present condition, they were ever designed to need the freedom of Dress that is so evident to the physical philosopher. The very length of the Dress produces these results if it is not tight around the body, for it must be remembered, that, even if the clothing is all suspended from the shoulders, the pressure upon the muscles there, press upon other muscles below, and they in turn upon others, and so the very same results are produced, only to a less extent, and requiring a longer time to feel the deleterious effects.

There cannot be perfect freedom of motion with the stockings arranged as they are;—the wearing of elastic bands either above or below the knee to keep them in position, prevents a perfect freedom of the motion of the legs, and even if the strap of Demorest notoriety is worn and fastened to a band from the waist, or to a waist itself, there is a want of freedom above, a compressing of muscles that injure a woman, as such, in a thousand-fold ratio.

The shoes are wretchedly constructed, preventing a freedom of motion by compressing some portion of the feet. Instead of the Horace Greeley style of the shoe being made to fit the foot, the foot is compressed so as to fit the shoe. The high heels are not only objectionable on account of the want of freedom of motion when they are worn, but a few words must here be added in regard to the women's weaknesses that are produced by placing the body in the wrong position and thus aggravating those diseases and displacements that are peculiar to women, wearing the ordinary style of dress; a full explanation of which, cannot be given to the public, save in a work especially devoted to the causes and preventives of the terrible conditions of the women of civilization.

## EQUAL DISTRIBUTION OF CLOTHING

The clothing should be equally distributed over the body, in order to enjoy perfect health; and when we realize how much of wretchedness is caused in the marriage relation that is the direct result of sickness of wife and children, we shall be prepared to understand what Dress Reform and Marriage have to do with each other; and when we go still farther, and show how much the equal distribution of the clothing of woman has to do with the morals of the world, both in marriage and out of it, the great hearts of the philanthropists will work with new zeal in a reform that is paramount in importance to anything before the Christian world. But the moral part of this part of the subject cannot be fully discussed, save in the woman's book, alluded to; the logical mind will, however, draw conclusions that cannot be far from the truth.

Not only is it necessary that the clothing should be equally distributed over the limbs and body for comfort, but the necessities of the circulation of the blood are such, that there is a demand for the same. There must be a certain and uniform warmth of the blood, not only to circulate well, but to gather up the waste material of the system as it courses its way. Chilblains and corns are caused because there is not a freedom and warmth of the circulation, so that the waste material can be gathered up by the blood, and thrown off through the various means that Nature has provided for the purpose.

If some part of the body is chilled, that part cannot throw off through insensible perspiration the worn-out particles that are constantly being eliminated by that process. And if the opposite extreme is the case, as where there is a heated condition of some portion, it cannot get rid of its effete material because there is a congested condition. There cannot be a local disease of any part of the system, (save by injury) unless there is a disturbance in the circulation of the blood, and if we will compare facts of the past with those of the present, we will find that there never was so many cases of rheumatism and neuralgia in the legs of women as while large hoops were worn. The limbs were so poorly protected, and the cold air circulated so freely around them, that the arterial blood was chilled before reaching the extremities, and then, in the returning venous circulation, running up against the laws of gravitation, the red rivers were wearied and dammed in their course.

Cold expels the blood while warmth invites it; and if the lower extremities suffer from a deficiency of the life current, the other parts of the body must suffer from an excess. Hence those who habitually have cold and chilly surfaces, have internal congestions, as in agues or chill fevers. Those who have flushed faces are troubled with cold feet, and before these subjects were as well understood as now, physicians believed, and enforced such belief with the lancet, that in all congestions there must of necessity be *too much* blood in the patient, instead of being an inequality in its circulation.

The various theories of the all healers, point directly to the equalizing of a disturbed circulation, although the advocates of Russian and Turkish baths, of movements, of electricity, of exercise, etc. etc. seldom explain, and do not always know, how much the wretched inequality of the distribution of the clothing of women has to do with the diseases and debility, not only of themselves, but of their little ones who do not live out half their days. We will go farther, and affirm, that, to an astonishing degree, are the men of the country indebted to their mothers for the great liability to congestive and nervous diseases (as they are popularly termed) from which they suffer. To that mother whose clothing was not properly and equally distributed over her system as child, maid, and wife.

This is a big subject, and comprehends what is meant by "the sins of the parents being visited upon the children," whether they intend them as sins or not. This is especially true as regards the mother, for in a large sense, she gives or takes as she will, whether she is intelligent or ignorant, and the children are thrust into existence with what she gives, and without what she fails to give, sometimes, aye often, resulting in life-long agonies to her.

## VITALITY SHOULD NOT BE EXPENDED BY DRESS

It should be the object of Dress to *save* vitality, instead of expending it, in the foolish and wicked manner that fashion dictates. And especially should this be true in re-gard to the Dress of women; for those who are, or are to be the mothers of the race, need all that the best of dressing can save.

To be a mother, to give life to an immortal being, to say what sort of a body shall hold the casket that contains an emanation from the Deity, is a trust not to be lightly thought of; and the conditions of a good giving, to be in any way departed from, because of the applause of the thoughtless, or the scorn and contempt, and neglect of those who look upon life from a low standpoint.

Nothing but a thoroughly hygienic Dress, worn all through young girlhood, womanhood, and wifehood, will save the vitality of women for the various duties of life, and especially for the high duties of a maternity that shall do the greatest credit to herself and her children. By a properly arranged Dress, the vitality may be saved from climatic influences, that would otherwise have the most baneful effects.

The study should be to arrange it in a way that will require the least expenditure to carry about. It is just as absurd to have skirts falling to the ankles of women, as it was in the ancient days of warriors, to have their horses covered with blankets, so long that they could not move back without stepping upon them. But the absurdity is nothing to be compared with the loss of vitality to women, in the wearing of the flowing drapery.

No man would keep an ostler who would be so cruel as to leave a heavy harness on his horse all night, or all day when not in use, and yet the proportion of vitality would be less, that would be lost in the horse that was treated thus, than in his wife, who wears a flowing dress all day. In a word, a woman in the ordinary Dress, expends more vitality in wearing such Dress, than a horse does wearing his harness, even if it were never removed, except to curry and bathe him.

The machinist calculates how little power will serve his purpose, and if a ten horse-power engine will do so, he is not so absurdly foolish as to get one of twelve or fifteen horse-power to do his work just for the sake of having it seen that he has an engine of such power. He would be thus throwing away two or three horse-power for the sake of appearance to those who are neither wise or scientific, but are fond of show. And yet a machinist who did thus, would be two or five horse-power wiser than the woman who expends half or three quarters of her vitality in needlessly carrying about the surplus clothing that all women do carry, who are wearing the ordinary Dress that is thrust upon woman, as one that is "becoming her sphere," forgetting that Christ and the Apostles, and the Catholic Priests, and the Japanese and Chinese men wore, and those now living are wearing, Dresses that fall to the ankles, and sometimes even longer.

Woman expends so much of vitality in carrying about drygoods, it is no wonder that she is twitted of her littleness in everything else; it is no wonder that she is unable to do, and unwilling to attempt to do, anything out of the line of her drygoods avocation, for the chains that bind her are so strong, that exertion is a task that cannot be fully appreciated by men.

The nerves are the conductors of the vital or nervo-vital power that pervades all through to such an extent, that the point of a pin cannot be inserted anywhere without wounding a nerve, just as it is impossible to do so without puncturing a blood vessel. The nerves are given off from the brain and spinal column, and as the power derived from them is the great mover of the human piece of mechanism, it is simply a matter of economy and duty not to waste such power, when all that makes life desirable is so seriously affected by a wasteful and extravagant expenditure of this animal electricity. To save this for a better purpose than hauling drygoods, would be wise, while there are plenty of horses, oxen and mules, that can be employed for the purpose.

The expenditure of so much vitality as women lose, not only does not fail to injure themselves, but does not result in any possible good to any human being. The saving of the vast amount worse than thrown away, would be of permanent benefit to the possessor, and to all persons with whom associated, and especially in the marriage relation.

## DESCRIPTION OF THE AMERICAN REFORM DRESS

The linen is made with high neck and loose waist, and whole drawers, and long sleeves with wristbands attached; thus making a complete undersuit in one garment. The drawers are folded over the ankles and the stockings adjusted over the drawers, thus keeping the ankles warm and also keeping the stockings arranged without elastics or other bands, or any troublesome or injurious arrangement, most of which impede the circulation and produce varicose veins, and weariness in walking.

The pants are made like men's, and are either but-
toned to the waist of the undersuit or are arranged with
the usual suspenders. The dress is made to hang free of the
body, the waist and skirt of one piece like a sack coat, and
falling to the knees; thus preventing it being stepped upon
while descending stairs, or of becoming soiled in rainy
days—but principally because of a needed relief to women
from its shortness. Thus, for general wear but three gar-
ments are required.

Woolen, and canton flannel, and silk may be made the
same as the ordinary linen undersuits (with the exception
of wristbands) when the season makes more clothing necessary, and these can be worn either over or under the
linen; thus giving the required amount of warmth,
without great expenditure of vitality to carry the clothes
about, or of money to purchase them.

The time is coming when every woman will dress in
this style, for the *advantages* are too evident, to be much
longer overlooked.

# CHAPTER III

# TOBACCO

Tobacco poisons the happiness of domestic life. It has not only *prevented* some marriages, but in many cases destroyed the happiness of the marriage relation.

There is nothing in creation that is so loathed by those who do not use it, as is Tobacco in its various preparations. And still those who suffer from its fumes are often, from various reasons, heard to say that it is *not* disagreeable. Many young ladies have seemed to be indifferent as to gentlemen smoking in their presence, when it was not only *disgusting* to them, but their whole physical frame suffered from its poisonous effects. It was not only a dread of offending those whose esteem they desired, but an undefined sort of a hesitancy, at commencing the discussion of a subject that they were not able to bring any arguments *against*, save their own disgust and bad physical effects, which they divined would be called "only a notion," and they be censured with a desire to dictate.

Many a lady has married a "mild Tobacco user," who was not herself aware of the depth of her disgust for the weed, until she found the restraints of society thrown off by her husband, and Tobacco used freely by him.

Some young ladies, while receiving the addresses of their affianced, dare to argue the case, and almost invariably are assured, that they "will use no more Tobacco after marriage."

But sad it is for poor human nature, that has contracted this habit, for the husband finds how next to impossible it is, to dispense with what he has become habituated to, and censures the wife with a want of *love for him*, if she is unwilling he should promote his happiness by *simply smoking!* If it is disagreeable to her he will not smoke in her presence. The young trusting wife, who believed when she had forsaken all for him, and he had promised not to "smoke any more," that he would keep his word, especially when it was *only to leave off smoking*, began to realize that he thought more of his Tobacco than his wife, more of his Tobacco than his promise; and she began to regret having married. She could not meet him with a smile, for when there are no smiles in the heart, there can be none in the face.

The husband thinks he has got a very selfish wife, and besides, she does not smile as she used to, and he has been deceived in her genial soul.

The wife's eyes are often dim with tears, as she says half aloud—O! I wonder if the men are *all* so selfish, that they *will smoke*, when they know how sickening it is to their wives? His breath is *so bad*, and his clothes are all full of the odor, and even in the washtub, and in the ironing room, one cannot pass the doors without catching something of the odor! O, if he only *would not smoke*, or if I only *could* endure it! But my heart is broken—he, yes, *he promised so faithfully* that he *"would not smoke any more!"* and now, when I am married to him, and *must* stay, I am to be tormented all the rest of my life with Tobacco! O dear, dear, what would I give if I were only single again, and at my own home, where I would be out of all traces of Tobacco?

Years pass away, and one child after another is added to the family, with such susceptibilities, that the poor mother has but little sleep or rest. Every little noise awakens and frightens them, and their little hearts will throb with fear at slight causes.

One who could see no other species of intemperance but that of intoxicating drinks, and see no necessity for a total abstinence from anything else, would wonder how it *happened* that a little child should be so nervous. While one fully understanding the terrible effects of Tobacco upon the system is led to wonder how it can be possible, that intelligent men can see the results of Tobacco-using, on wife and children, and never trace such effects to the true cause.

One person cannot sleep with another who uses Tobacco, or even in the same room, without feeling the effects of the poison. There is a lassitude, a general debility, a want of energy, an irritability, a defective memory; all of which are the results of the poisonous Tobacco, with

which the air of the room is filled, being constantly ex-
haled from the lungs, and also thrown off by insensible
perspiration. I am aware that some will attempt to reason
that it is only the carbon that produces these effects, and
will bring in the sophistry of two or three physicians (who
are slaves to the pipe) to prove that the poisonous Tobacco
is "brain food, and does not injure any one when used
properly in a moderate manner." Such false teachings
however are not believed by even the most ignorant and
vile, for they have too much reason not to see the baneful
effects, but are too great slaves to break their weedy chains,
just as are the men referred to, who try to defend their
own vile habits.

The most scientific people in this country and abroad,
deprecate the use of Tobacco on the ground of its injurious effects.

It is really painful to see a physician's mind so clouded
with smoke, that he will not only attempt to justify its use,
but also to prescribe the same as a remedy. Such a one
ought to be sent to a lunatic asylum, for the purpose of
having the smoke extracted from his brain, to make room
for more knowledge of materia-medica.

Happy marriages have been made wretched by the
ignorance or the bigotry of a physician, who gravely made
a prescription of Tobacco, to be smoked or chewed a certain number of times per day. It is just as much a crime, for
a medical adviser to recommend Tobacco, as it is for a clergyman to recommend larceny. If there is a difference in the
degree of the crime, the clergyman's sin is the lesser.

The sufferings of the wife of a Tobacco-user, are often greater, and certainly more constant, and agonizing, than are those of the thief. In the case of the one, the good name is injured, but there are noble souls who sympathize with her, and feel that she is not to blame for her husband's evil deeds, while with the other a thousand wrongs to soul and body that cannot be told must be silently endured!

The use of Tobacco generates thirst, and if the father does not resort to the cup, he drinks large quantities of other stimulating fluids, thus weakening digestion. If the digestion is weakened, the whole nervous system is weakened, for it is by the food being properly digested and assimilated, that the nerves are nourished. Not only this, but the poison reaches every tissue in the body, producing under some circumstances the greatest excitability of the system, and under others a stolid indifference.

The children suffer from weak digestion, and morbid tastes. The brain suffers and the memory is impaired. The little minds are far from being what they would have been, had not the father's "mouth been a nicotine distillery."

Tobacco cannot be used in any form, without producing evil effects, mentally or physically, sooner or later, upon the user, the wife and the children. America would do well to copy one of the cantons of Switzerland, where an edict has been issued, forbidding any youth under eighteen to smoke, for, with the inborn depraved tastes of the boys of to-day, and the bad examples before them, it is a terrible fact, that boys but six or seven years of age, from the position of bootblack up, are seen in our streets smoking. They are to be the future husbands of the loved and cherished little angel daughters that you treat so tenderly. What of their marriage? Fathers, will you blind your eyes, continue to smoke or chew yourselves, and give all your influence in favor of what has destroyed the happiness of your own marriage relation?

It is gratifying to know that there are those who look upon this subject in some of its true lights, and it is to be hoped that some effectual measures may be instituted, to prevent the extending of such a terrible evil. It was noticed in the public press, that, as long since as 1860, the French Minister of Public Instruction published a circular, addressed to the directors of colleges and schools in France, *forbidding* the use of Tobacco in any form, by the students, on the ground that its use checked the physical and intellectual development. The Chamberlain of London found that many petty crimes were committed by boys in consequence of their using Tobacco.

Does Tobacco have nothing to do with the marriage relation, when the poor mother's heart is saddened with the thought that her boy is being ruined from using what may prevent, not only his mental and physical growth, but also make him a criminal? We quote the following from "a torn scrap of a leaf."

"Tobacco has utterly spoiled and ruined thousands of boys. It tends to the softening and weakening of the bones, and it greatly injures the brain, the spinal marrow, and the whole nervous fluid. A boy who smokes early and frequently, or in any way uses large quantities of Tobacco, is never known to make a man of much energy, and generally lacks muscular and physical, as well as mental power. We would particularly warn boys, who want to be anything in the world, to shun Tobacco as a most baneful poison." "The laws of health are infallible; the relation between transgression and the penalty is invariable, and the infliction of the latter is certain to follow upon the former. There is nothing about which young persons are more beguiled and deluded, than the belief that they can transgress natural laws, and jump the penalty. Punishment for a violation of natural law is just as certain as that the sun itself shines, and one cannot violate a law of his being, or any part of it, that there is not registered in him a penalty."

Tobacco often produces, not only paralysis, but insanity. We will introduce but one case of the former, and one of the latter, although it would be an easy matter to show that much of the insane immorality, and much of the paralysis that is becoming so frequent, and destroying the peace of the marriage relation, is due to Tobacco.

While in Paris, the author was called to see a case of paralysis, of a number of years standing, where both of the legs were affected to such a degree that the gentleman had not been in the street for several years. He was an inveterate Tobacco-smoker, as his wife informed her. The other case is as follows:

"Some twelve months ago a young man who was then employed in the Nashville and Decatur Railroad car shops, a steady, industrious mechanic, formed the acquaintance of a lady about fifteen years of age, who resided a few miles from the city. An attachment speedily sprang up between the two, which resulted in an engagement.

"Their first troubles arose from the objections urged by the parents of the young lady. The old folks preferred another man. In anticipation of his marriage however, the suitor had saved from his wages a considerable amount of money. He could now give the object of his affection a comfortable home, and saw no reason for waiting.

"He asked that the wedding might take place at an early day, but his *fiancée* wished to defer the nuptials for two months, as at the expiration of that time she would be sixteen. This, with renewed opposition from the parents, seems to have weighed heavily upon his mind. He was an inveterate chewer of Tobacco, and had often consumed nearly half a pound per day. This habit had long been at work undermining his nervous system, and his sorrows made him all the more persistent in masticating the weed. His quid was his constant companion. The more he thought of his crossed love, the harder he chewed. There was no limit to his unnatural indulgence. Every sight was suggestive of a fresh mouthful.

"The rest is soon told. About two weeks since, he began to exhibit unmistakable signs of lunacy, and is now in a Lunatic Asylum. His mental condition is directly attributed by the physicians to the excessive use of tobacco, aggravated by the effects of disappointed love on a weakened intellect."

But aside from the bad effects of Tobacco on temper and mind and body, the family is often deprived of actual necessaries, because of its expense. It is not enough to send the poisonous smoke into lungs of families, containing, as it does, *prussic acid*, but the very atmosphere is impregnated to such an extent, that it is almost intolerable. It is consumed to an alarmingly fearful extent. The following is an estimate in one city alone.

"WASTED IN SMOKE.—It is estimated that 20,000 cigars are daily sold on Broadway, New York, of which one twentieth cost 30 cents, two twentieths 25 cents, one fifth 20 cents, two fifths 15 cents, and one fourth 10 cents; making $3,300 a day, or $1,204,500 a year for cigars on that single street. It is also estimated that 75,000,000 cigars are consumed in the city, at a cost of $9,650,000. This, with the amount annually expended for pipes and tobacco, makes an aggregate of $10,500,000, yearly consumed in smoke in this city."

If all this $10,500,000 was expended in providing homes and food for the worthy poor, and unfortunately degraded women of New York, thousands of agonies would be relieved, and millions more prevented. Think for a moment of the smoke inhaled from the burning of 75,000,000 of cigars, to say nothing about the pipes, and then wonder at the great number of cases of throat and lung diseases, which all intelligent members of the Medical Profession know are aggravated, and often produced by Tobacco smoke.

Think how next to impossible it is to remain in a single house twenty-four hours, without being compelled to inhale the poisonous odor, for the atmosphere is so filled with the same that you cannot find *even a breath* of the pure element (so essential to health) only occasionally, when "the wind is so high" that men can not smoke in the streets, and you are so fortunate as to be in a house, where your near neighbors do not send the poison through the crevices. Talk of a wife being amiable, when the poisonous smoke stings every nerve as sensibly as though pins and needles were her torturers! As well might you talk of her being amiable under the one infliction, as under the other, if she is of a sensitive organization. If you have a complaint to make against such *effects*, you must remember that the author did not originate the law of effects.

That the same cause produced nettles and ivy, that produced Tobacco, no one will doubt, but that mankind ought to smoke or chew them, and believe they were intended for such purposes, simply *because* they *grow*, no sensible person would listen to for a moment; and yet we hear Tobacco-users undertake to defend its use, on the ground that "God made Tobacco for some purpose, and that purpose was just what it is so extensively used for." As well might we undertake to say that God made hemp to grow, for the purpose of hanging his creatures! Civilization has found that such a use of *hemp* is a perversion of God's laws, and the time *will* come when it will be as clearly seen that the present use of Tobacco is just as *much* a perversion of *His* laws.

In the grand march of the human intellect, the true use for which Tobacco was intended will be discovered in the chemical or manufacturing arts. Until that time it ought to be classed with nettles and ivy.

In 1865 the total amount of internal revenue from Tobacco and its manufacture was $11,387,799. If the labor in producing and manufacturing and in gathering the revenue, had been expended in raising food, or taking the wealth from the mines of our country of "inexhaustible resources," who could find language to picture the happiness that would have resulted in the marriage relation of many thousands? There ought to be no reason why every family in America should be without a neat little home of their own; and if it were not for the vices that are indulged in, no one would ever exclaim,

> "No foot of land do I possess,
> No cottage in this wilderness,"

where I can sing

> "Home, sweet home."

# CHAPTER IV

# TEMPERANCE

"Strong drink is raging, and whosoever is deceived thereby is not wise." The intoxicating cup is destroying the happiness of the marriage relation in nearly sixty thousand families every year in the United States. It is surprising, with all the intelligence extant, that we should have such a record!

The beauties of Total Abstinence are so plain to be seen, and they are so evident to the most casual observer, that it is really surprising that there should be any necessity, for ever having another chapter written upon the subject. The theme itself has been worn threadbare, and yet great armies are constantly committing suicide, instead of nobly fighting the battles of life, without laying the armor down, until the frosts of years shall invite a slumber beneath the sods, that must sometime be the counterpane on a bed, that Deity shall alternately make white with snow, and perfume with roses.

The most charming of all things earthly, is the thought of dying a beautiful death, and seeing just how the soul leaves the casket that has identified it with mortality, and how it shall catch the first *grand*, aye *sublime* scenery of Eternity! But, if delirium tremens, or apoplexy, or softening of the brain, or death of any kind, in an unnatural condition of the God-mind within, takes the soul out of the shackles of Time into the freedom of Eternity, the exquisite pleasure of witnessing that but *once* transition, is lost forever, and the pangs of one of the "broken-pair," when such a death is remembered, must assuredly detract from many an hour of happiness.

Think how many families have suffered by deaths from Intemperance—how many marriages been severed! In 1826, when the United States had but twelve millions of people, fifty-six million gallons of intoxicating beverages were consumed annually; the announcement of which, startled the people so much, that at the close of 1829 a thousand Temperance organizations were formed, having one hundred thousand names who had signed the pledge.

But not until the great work commenced, had but few formed anything like a correct idea of the want, misery, *agony*, of the drunkards' wives and children.

Temperance societies have increased since then, until they are vast in numbers, and thousands of sorrows assuaged and prevented, in the marriage relation. But thousands more have existed all this time, and the effects on soul and body, and mind, are to be seen every day, whichever way we turn.

At this hour wives and children are drinking cups of *agony*, to their very dregs, just as deep and bitter, as wife or child ever sipped! *We* in our enlightenment, right in the face of these facts, have stepped away back of even the people of *Burmah*, for one of their "five moral codes" says, "Thou shalt use no intoxicating liquors." and *Christians* at every County Fair, and State Fair, appoint a Committee to test *domestic wines*, made out of currants, gooseberries, elderberries, raspberries, and cherries. And because they are made of fruits that we have always been accustomed to eating freely, they reason that it "must of necessity be harmless, when they are *only the juices of fruits?*"

They seem to forget that imported wine is *only the juice of grapes*, and all other liquors, *only the juice of grains*; and on this *truthfully-false* basis, premiums are awarded to those who succeed in making the most deliciously fine poisons. Temperate men expatiate upon the economy, and purity of the same, in comparison with foreign wines, and thus the whole country is encouraged to make and use that which will assuredly undermine both the mental and physical foundations.

It is not necessary to use liquors of any kind to the extent that will produce entire, or even partial intoxication, to make a great amount of wretchedness, for the little that causes irritability, often makes more real and continuous unhappiness in the marriage relation, than when used to that excess which results in entire unconsciousness. The *happiness-exterminator* produces its effects in so many ways, and shades of varieties of ways, that "every heart knows its own sorrows," better than can ever be portrayed by another individual.

The various temperaments, and their thousand different combinations—the various grades of intelligence, natural or acquired—the various ideas of just the amount of abuse men can with impunity heap upon women, and escape punishment from law or from public sentiment, are such that no writer or speaker can do justice in attempting to portray them. The unending sorrows that are of such a nature that common delicacy forbids to mention, seem almost beyond the reach of a remedy, from the fact, that such *cannot be heralded to the world.* When an allusion is made to them, those not victims, cannot believe in so great a depravity of *sober men!*

The great reason why these wrongs are not trumpeted, is because those who make them, are constantly crying down what they term "very unfit stuff for the public," and endeavoring to keep up a sentiment that will not allow the dissemination of unvarnished facts, in relation to such wrongs, not only, but to create a still greater intolerance, if possible. The surface, and some of the very depths, of the sorrows to tipplers' wives, have been panoramically placed before the public, but were the scenes "behind the curtain" only unrolled, others would see them as they are in reality.

Could all the smiles that are from other causes than to cover sorrows, be measured, one would be but poorly supported who was paid for measuring, while the one who weighed the sorrow-covering-ones would almost need some fortified tower to deposit the gains. Undefined wrongs are always the worst to fight, and it is only by agitation, that their heinousness is seen sufficiently clear to call forth efforts necessary in the case.

No one can be found who cannot see the great wrongs resulting from excessive drinking, for they are so defined, that there is no mistaking them. Families of such have a sympathy, which helps them to endure their sorrows, but they feel, notwithstanding, that "*somebody* is to blame" for allowing even the *sale* of intoxicating beverages, if not their manufacture or distillation.

It is the opinion of some of those learned in the Medical Profession that eating stimulating food creates such a thirst for stimulating drinks, that the one will never be permanently abandoned until the other is also, at least among the masses of the people. This may be true if only moral suasion shall be used. The Royal Family of Prussia seem to have some correct and advanced ideas on this subject, for sugar plums, rich food, wines and beer are never allowed their children.

It is surprising that all intelligent people do not see that what is not good for a child—what will not help to *make* the mature individual—cannot be essential to life. Poverty, and ten thousand sorrows that make life a wretched state of existence, result to families, because the husband and father *will* indulge in that which can intoxicate.

A drink, has in many cases changed the position of a lifetime; but of the cases recorded there is not one perhaps, so very striking as the consequences of one drink. The Duke of Orleans, the eldest son of Louis Philippe, King of the French, was the inheritor of whatever rights the royal family could transmit. On one occasion he invited a few companions to take breakfast with him, as he was about to leave Paris to join his regiment. In the conviviality of the hour he drank too much wine. He did not become intoxicated; he was not in any respect a dissipated man; but he drank a glass too much, and lost the balance of his body and mind. Bidding adieu to his companions he entered the carriage. But for that extra glass he would have kept his seat; he leaped from the carriage; his head struck the pavement; he was taken into a beer shop and died. That glass of wine overthrew the Orleans dynasty, confiscated their property of $100,000,000, and sent the whole family into exile.

The hundreds of thousands of bushels of grains and fruits that are *worse than wasted* every year, to make the soul and body destroying beverages, would, if given to the poor, or sold to them at a small price, prevent the half famished from stealing or of dying of want. It is not because there is not an enormous and all sufficient quantity of the most nutritious food raised every year, that it is so hard to keep soul and body together respectably, but because of the *wicked destruction* of such food, by converting the same into poisonous beverages.

Government allows the poison to be made; and it licenses men to sell it to the people, and then it licenses Lawyers to defend those who commit crimes while under the effects of such poison, and it pays Policemen to watch them, and builds jails and prisons to confine the unruly, and pays Doctors to give opiates to those on the verge of delirium tremens. It gives them food because it does not dare to starve them to death. It takes them to Courts and tries them, and pays Jurors and Judges, and is at all sorts of expenses for its *first folly of allowing the poison to be manufactured.*

But what of the families of these men, all this time? Need the picture be painted on this page, when it is seen in all the vivid colors of naturalness in thousands of tenements, from brown-stone fronts to the poorest hovels! Government is altogether too dignified an institution, to look farther into the matter than to build poor-houses for the wives and children. And so the world moves on, and it must needs be through individual benevolence, that insane asylums are spoken into existence, to treat those who have lost their reason in consequence of trouble that has been caused by the effects of Intemperance.

Husbands may outrage every sense of decency while in a partial state of intoxication, and Lawyers will take a little wine just before they make a plea for or against them. Judges must leave their benches to drink a glass of old Bourbon, and the Jury cannot decide upon grave cases, without being *stimulated*, and no one seems to think that a *degraded criminal needs* any of the *stuff* to sustain him; O no, *he* has had a *little*—just a *trifle too much*; and so the dignitaries are showing him just how much it is *proper* to take!

Everybody sees men who make and execute laws "taking a little," and so if they ever expect to be great, they must follow in the steps of the illustrious.

A number of years since, a man, while in a partially

intoxicated condition, hired a dentist for $80, to extract all of his wife's teeth; but he had sufficient reason left, so that he gave the ether, and told the wife, Frances B. Norris, that he would kill her if she told of it. Every tooth was not only sound, but double.

Every few weeks we read an account of a man killing his wife, or butchering his children, while under the effects of the poison that our great Government derives such a large internal revenue from. But all *women* cannot resist the temptations to taste as well as look upon the sparkling wine, and so they degrade themselves, and sink lower and lower into haunts of vice, with the cup to encourage and strengthen them in their dens of iniquity. It is rare indeed to find a woman who is lost to all moral sense, that does not tip the bottle.

Hundreds of families who mourn the loss of a charming daughter, "*that is worse than dead*," well know that the cup has dealt a double draught of poison, to *them* and *her*. Neither pen nor brush can ever do justice to the subject in portraying the real condition of families, where the intoxicating cup has found an honored place.

# CHAPTER V

# WOMAN'S FRANCHISE

With woman's enfranchisement comes her unqualified individuality. Without it, just so much, or so little, as men choose to allow her; and that allowance is according to the preconceived opinions, or prejudices, of the men with whom she is related.

The different measures of justice to woman, is according to circumstances, or in the English way of speaking, "it depends"—none of these measures *full*, save in a few instances, where laws, or the want of laws, would not make any material difference with them.

God has given to woman just as defined and important rights of individuality, as He has to man; and any man-made laws that deprive her of any rights or privileges, that are enjoyed by himself, are usurpations of power. Such laws are an outrage, and as much a contravention of God's laws, as though man deprived woman of her life; for her aspirations and freedom of soul, are as dear to her as is her life.

Deity intended a free and full development of all of woman's powers, as well as man's, and gave her a mind to decide for herself in all things. There are thousands of cases on every hand, where more wretchedness, aye, *agony*, would be prevented by man's taking woman's *life* from her, than taking liberties that the Franchise would secure to her. The mass of men do not see this, as they are too apathetic to do so, for all men are not so selfish that they would not see and help to right the wrongs of woman, if the subject were presented to them so that they truly felt her position.

Man not having been deprived of his individuality, does not know the feeling of degradation, that a woman experiences, and how her soul writhes under the chains that have inscribed upon them, "thus far and no farther," *because you are a woman.* Why should there be anything said about what shall be the bounds of a woman's abilities, or where shall be the limits, any more than those of a man? He is free to make of himself what he is capable of doing, and no one is expected to interfere in his plans, *because he is a man enfranchised.*

It is not surprising that there are a thousand covered wrongs where the victims and their friends see no remedy from exposure; but they do see disgrace from acts that they had not a particle of control over, not only, but before years, and the knowledge that comes with them, were theirs. The personal violence on little girls, as young as four or five years, has been known in dozens of instances, by men old enough to be their fathers. The trickery and deception of artful men, and young and trusting maidens, clearly prove that the individuality of woman has no recognition, but that she should be the toy and tool of man, and thus the victims are compelled to acknowledge the superiority of a brute force, that would not have been let loose, but for the ideas of a woman's rights of perfect individuality having been ignored.

No man fully believing in the enfranchisement of women, would be guilty of such crimes, and if any pretender to such principles has been, it is because some sinister motives have led him to the advocacy of principles, the very nature of which, would lead to a practical recognition of justice. The recognition of the individuality of woman, is simply an acknowledgment of human rights, which all human beings have guaranteed them, by the fact of their having an existence; as surely is this, as is the right to exist at all.

Every age sighs over the injustice of the men to women, in former ages, or among a certain people, and are proud of progress in this direction in their own time. Our men of to-day in the United States boast of more individuality for woman, than in any age or country. Who can be found that does not denounce the people who kill their parents so soon as they become old and useless? And yet the young women have been so deprived of individuality, that they are seen when old, often in a prison of a poorhouse, or shivering over a few apples or matches on the corners of streets, while their *protectors*, men, walk by unmoved, and loudly prating about women having more rights than themselves, while they are at the same time their slaves and protectors and providers.

Until God has taken from woman the greatest token of an individual, that he could by any possibility have given her, that is, not only the right of going out of life into the great eternity alone,—but the impossibility of having a man to act for her, or even to accompany her through the valley and shadow of death, (what the Hindoo husband fears so much, that he compels his wife to go with him,) not until then, should man assume even more than Deity Himself.

The great mass of men seem not to have thought that a woman stands in intimate relations to human rights as well as themselves, and yet they censure her if she does not assume all, in the sphere that they have marked out—*all* that the dictators decide to belong to said *sphere*.

Men do not respect women who do not respect their own individuality. They may not have the sickly sentiment of sham or pretended respect, which is so transitory, for those who are individualized, that they do for those who are *not*, but while they hate the women of metal, they cannot fail to *respect*.

No woman can sacrifice individuality, for gold or love, or anything whatever, without losing, in the very act, all that would be worth a purchase or a gift. The mass of women who do this, are either indolent, or are living

222222222

objectless lives. It is true that some are indolent because of physical inability, for the construction of woman's clothing is such that she cannot be otherwise. Some are living objectless lives, because they see how terrible the battles that must be waged, if they live to some purpose in what would be tasteful to them. There are a thousand things that man does not see the whys and wherefores, simply because he has not fought the world with a woman's obstacles to surmount, or perish.

Some women do not wish to be enfranchised, because their husbands or fathers are in some positions that are for life, and they will be pensioned after such *supporter's* death, and they are so wanting in benevolence to others, that they are perfectly regardless of the interests of others, so long as they are provided for themselves.

*Ignorance* or *selfishness* covers the whole ground of the opposition to woman being enfranchised, whether it comes from woman or man.

That the Political equality of the sexes will produce radical changes in society generally and the marriage relation specially, is evident to all. Men have felt this in a poignant degree, and so great has been their fear that they will lose their assumed power over woman as *wife*, that they have opposed even the *discussion* of the subject, unless it has been in the presence of those who were so little in the habit of arguing in a logical manner, that they had no fears that their wives, or those they *hoped* to be such, would be likely to get "woman's rights notions into their heads."

Men have from time to time made concessions to

woman in the statutes, for the purpose of quieting those who were restless under great wrongs; but it has always been with an argument upon their lips, that "women were better off than men; that they were better protected by law, and had *more rights* than men, under the law." And they have labored to make them feel, that, *because* the power was in their hands to make laws more just to themselves, and because they had given these *privileges* to women, the women ought to feel under the greatest of obligations to them. They have conceded with the one hand, and chained with the other, and then charged women with the greatest of *ingratitude* if she dared to complain that the chains were too grievous to be borne!

Twenty years ago, scarcely a man could be found who could hear the words "woman's rights," without immediately becoming angry. His usurpation of the God-given rights of woman to her own person, he saw at a glance would be endangered, and if *allowed* to come up fairly and squarely, would in time take from man his assumed power to act the petty tyrant in the household over his wife.

Men do not come out boldly and declare that the *real* ground of their opposition to the Franchise of woman, is as we have stated, for they well know that it would be an acknowledgment that the greatest of wrongs to soul and body of woman, were now inflicted without her having the power to prevent them.

Those men who are prating so loudly that if women have the *Ballot* in their hands, the marriage relation will be in time ignored, and the homes all destroyed, are men who in *reality* are not honestly afraid that such a condition of affairs will result; but they *are* afraid that public sentiment will be so purified, that they will not be tolerated in decent society, if they are not as pure as they now demand their wives to be, and accord to woman the same rights in all social and Political affairs, which they arrogate unto themselves because they are *men*.

Thousands of women's hearts are at this very hour echoing the sentiments just expressed, and if they were not so bound down that they have lost the power to *dare* express themselves on this subject, the cry of *"it's true, it's true!"* would not only be heard from the great mass of women, but our halls where we are having quiet and orderly discussions, would be one vast scene of confusion, where the great and agonizing wrongs of the marriage relation would burst forth from the lips of women, in voices a thousand strong at once! They would not allow us, who have been so many years pleading their cause and acting their representatives, to keep back the great reason of *all* reasons, why men oppose woman's equality with them at the Ballot-box.

Here and there are found women who can hardly hold their peace, but are afraid to enter into a discussion that they feel themselves incompetent to close, with full credit to themselves, because, while their ideas are clear, and connected, and logical *in* their brains, their long servile condition, and the terrible ridicule meted out to them, prevent them from taking them *out* of their brains.

Men may attempt to turn the great question in other directions, and give other reasons why they oppose the

enfranchisement of woman. They may talk of her unfitness
for office, and of her crowding *men* out of position. They
may talk about the children and homes being so neglected
if women go to the polls once a year to vote. They may
get up all the hobgoblins and side issues that their brains
are capable of manufacturing, but still, the great question
that underlies the whole, is the *loss* of assumption of power
over the wife.

It is plain to be seen that they would yield everything
that woman demands, if the tyranny as *husband* could be
saved. This is *the* question that underlies all others, and she
who now speaks, expects nothing but abuse from such
men, and even some women, who do not themselves
understand the great question, or do not dare be full expo-
nents of principles, that the sham modest cannot open to
the public. She has dared for twenty years to advocate and
live principles in the face of a tyrannical public sentiment,
and the time has come when she *does not dare* walk all
around the question, as some others do, and thus postpone
for many years, the agitation of the *real* question at issue.

Men know that the time has passed, that they can, in
America, control the *minds* of women successfully, and
now the time is almost at hand, when they will be unable
to control the *bodies*. The great mass of men are to-day
assuming to be lords over women, and the great mass of
women deny any such *right*, and hence the quarrel.

Had woman Political equality, she would also have
social equality, and if she had social equality, the great
causes for bickerings would be removed, and thus the mar-

riage relation would, as a natural consequence, be bettered. Men would no more attempt to coerce their wives to think or act according to their own ideas or wishes, than they would *other* women. They would not assume any rights of control on the ground of the marriage relation.

One human being has no right to assume control over another, and the smallest of all *mean smallnesses*, is that which is assumed by the husband over the wife, because of his greater physical strength, and her political weakness. Suppose that principle were carried out into all the relations of life, and every man who met another, weaker *physically* than himself, should rob him of all his money, and threaten to "kill him if he told of it;" men would soon see that physical strength ought not to be the criterion to judge the God-given rights of human beings.

There are great wrongs in all countries in relation to the marriage question, which can *never* be righted, until woman shall stand side by side with man, as an equal in the legislating. The most important of all laws that come within the sphere of legislation, are the *Marriage* laws; and until woman has a voice in making them, they must of necessity be imperfect, as are all laws, where physical force is required to execute them, and woman has had no voice in their making.

To say that the happiness of the marriage relation is not affected by oppressive laws that make women wretched, in such relation, would be to make an affirmation glaringly false. Where the most *just* laws are enacted, there are the happiest marriages. The most *unjust* are found where the wife is caught and *compelled* to live in such a relation; as is the case in the South Sea Islands, where "woman's influence in politics" in any shape, would be considered to be much farther out of "her sphere," than the Ballot is by the most ignorant in America.

The shortest-sighted can readily see the relation the Ballot would have to social life, in such a degraded condition as in the Isles just referred to. It could hardly be possible to find an individual, who made any pretence of possessing intelligence, who would not acknowledge that the Ballot, even if in the hands of but *half* the people, would be instrumental in making much better laws for the other half, than where there was no people's Ballot. In such a case, those who were at all disposed to mete out a respectable measure of justice, would be much more likely to do so. It may be argued further, that if *all* the people helped to frame the laws, none but those who had the general good of society at heart, would attempt to speak otherwise than in this direction, and it would therefore follow that the greatest good would result to the many, and as the causes for dissensions in society generally would be in a great measure removed, so would the marriage relation be bettered in the same proportion.

*Equals* are not the ones to have dissensions of any magnitude as a rule, but the troubles of life arise mainly out of the *real* or *assumed* superiority of the one, on one side, and the assumed inferiority on the other. If a pugilist charges another with inferiority, the question is settled very soon by a trial of physical strength. And if two *minds* were to debate the question of mental power, they would not be so simple as to undertake to enforce their mental superiority by physical means. And yet in the marriage relation, without the majority of men seeming to realize it, they are doing so in regard to woman.

When men think more upon this subject they will be surprised at their own unjust ideas, which have so grown with them, that they have become a part of their very being. It cannot be denied that many are kind and very just according to *their own ideas* of those qualities. But the effects in many respects are the same as though there were different ruling motives.

But many wretched women do not ask for the Ballot. They do not want the right to *vote*, but they want simply the "rights that *women* ought to have, without meddling with politics, the business of men." They say this because they do not understand the relation that the Ballot has to them in their domestic wrongs. Poor martyrs, you would be able to right those wrongs if you had the Ballot in your hand, and the simple fact of your having the Ballot would carry with it a respect for your human rights.

Look at the late Negro slaves, and see the difference in their treatment, even in matters that are away beyond the sphere of Legislation! There would be just as noticeable a difference in the respect of man for woman. Struggle for *political rights*, for it is through such, and such alone, that you will ever obtain *human rights*. It is not simply for *yourself*, but for that great army of young women, who cannot yet see the necessity for anything but smiles and gallantry from the future husbands. We who are laboring for the enfranchisement of woman, represent the strongest of maternal natures, for we would protect the young and innocent, and the helpless everywhere, from encroachments, and the wrongs that result from physical force. Instead of being "*out of our spheres*," we are just *in* them, only in a wider, more important and more potent sense.

As a Physician, the author believes that her duties are not *all* in the sick-room, for, after an experience of over fifteen years, she finds herself loudly called to diagnose the great body politic, more thoroughly than ever before, and her prognosis is, that *doubling* the dose at the Ballot-box will produce convalescence. Every one knows that the people are happier when well, than when sick, and after the important dose has been taken and health secured, the marriage relation will be something better than the least binding contract that is ever made. There will be no such terrible *binding*, as in South Carolina, where no divorces are ever granted, no matter how terrible the wrongs, and where a man can by law give a certain portion of his property to his mistress, the same as though his wife were dead. Neither will Massachusetts and New York go to Indiana to right wrongs that never can be righted in their own States; for every State in the Union will have such just laws, that there will be no necessity for fleeing to the protection of another State.

Had woman a Ballot in her hand, there would not exist in any State such sham codes of morals, as are on our New York Statutes, where no divorces can be had except for the crime of adultery; which all know is, by the very nature of such crime, almost impossible to *prove*. Then, in another act, it takes away the *power* to prove the same, by not allowing the husband or wife to testify against each other, and *by* allowing the guilty parties to remain silent as regards their own crimes. Those who are not guilty, could with an honest face testify, while those who are, ought to be made to testify accordingly, and have the severest punishment for perjury enforced, if the latter crime were added to the former.

New York, and all States with such tyrannical laws, show that they do not wish to be just, or have not the ability to frame equitable laws, or are afraid that they are powerless to enforce them. Any one reason is a disgrace to a great State. But when the plea for the continuance of such laws, is, that it is to "promote morality that stringent divorce laws are still on the Statutes," the idea is too absurd for serious arguments, were it not for the terrible wrongs that are constantly resulting to the *best* citizens, while the *worst* pursue the vilest course of life under legal cover.

Women, those who are neither idiots nor criminals in any respect, are the greater sufferers from such laws. It is true that the same State prohibits the one who is divorced, from ever marrying again, while the one who obtains a divorce, is at liberty to do so—but at the same time, if it be a *woman*, it sends her into a house of ill fame, as public sentiment will not allow her to have a *shelter*, it hardly matters *what* were the circumstances connected with the case. She is deprived of every dollar of the property she may have helped to indirectly accumulate by serving and saving, and she is turned into the street characterless, moneyless, friendless, without health, to beg, starve, or sell herself. Begging will not avail, for she has not as fair a chance as the filthiest vagabond. If she were able to work, no man who would not sink her still lower in his selfish purposes, will employ her—woman who has a sympathy for her condition does not dare employ her, because "she will disgrace her house," and so if she prefers to live in a disreputable house, where she has some voice in the rent of her body, instead of dying in the street, where perhaps she would have no voice in the matter, she does the best she can under the circumstances, and the men who *made* the laws that sent her there, and the men who *execute* the laws, visit her until she becomes too degraded for *respectable gentlemen*.

This is one of the degraded women that we hear just such men talk about exercising the rights of Franchise with their wives and daughters, if women are "allowed to vote." These women are the legal *nonentities*, except when law can degrade. *Men*, the legal *protectors of women*, ask you what would be the condition of society, if all the women in certain houses were allowed to vote? but they do not ask us, what is the condition of society now that *all* the *men* who keep up such houses are voters!

But to return. If it be a *man* who is divorced, he simply pursues the same course of iniquity, and to carry out his tyrannical spirit, presents quibble after quibble to delay and annoy as long as it is *possible*, often for years and years; and when his legal oppression fails to compel her to condone, he brings charges against *her*, of the same character of which *he* is actually guilty. Having the purse-strings in his grasp, he buys up witnesses against himself, or sends them to parts not known, where they die, and the evidence is buried forever. He also buys witnesses to swear against a pure spirit they never saw, until in the Court-room; and if, after series of years and the pure one has waded through all the seas of law that can be brought to bear upon the case, and Justice extends her hand with the scroll of freedom, the scrawny fingers that receive it, must spend the best part of the remaining years in toil, to pay the costs of Courts and borrowed money that paid expenses to sea-sides, and mountains, and for journeys, that saved the poor victim from a lunatic asylum!

But it will be said men are *obliged* to pay all court expenses, and support the wife while getting a bill from him. Yes, if he *has* any money, and if she swears she does not know anything, and can't do anything to support herself, or is too sick to do so, the court will eke out something, according to *his* ideas of the case, and every body will pity the husband who has such an *apology* for a wife, little thinking that many who have gone to their graves, in consequence of such troubles, could not even survive *long enough*, to be living apologies for women, whose every look speaks of the terrible wrongs of man-made laws! Husbands are *obliged* to provide for wives who get a bill of Divorce. Yes, if they *have* any property, and if they have not taken it to another State, where it can't be reached by law, and if they do not manage to run away and change their names, and *if* and *if* and *if*!!

It is just as much the *duty* of Congress to make general laws respecting marriage and Divorce, as to make any other laws; and when we see the terrible effects of unrighteous laws on this world-wide discussed subject, and realize the importance of Marriage to the perpetuity, of an intelligent government, we can but believe that its necessity will not long be overlooked. The days are not distant when England will do this, and thus prevent more terrible cases of the Yelverton type, where a noble woman and her children are wronged for life.

But there is no necessity for our travelling thousands of miles from our native shores, to gather wrongs that result from the want of just and universal laws, in relation to marriage, for every month brings victims to the surface, that have been buried in injustice. Thousands of noble Sage-Richardsons are suffering this hour! Nothing but the Ballot in woman's hand will right these wrongs, by making just laws, wherein a pure marriage relation may be perpetuated, just as nothing but the power of woman in Legislative and Congressional halls, will perpetuate the Union of States.

As a last reason urged against the Ballot for women, we hear that they cannot be warriors, and defend a country, and therefore have no right to take part in a government. Such reasoners are always found to be either ignorant of the histories of past and present ages, or are selfish tricksters, who well know that they would never succeed in their plans if women were enfranchised. The instances of bravery, starvation, suffering, wounds and death of women both North and South during our late war, ought to forever close the mouths of such reasoners, even if wholly ignorant of the thousands of instances in all ages, of the never by man excelled courage, bravery, endurance and patriotism, of the women of the past. The following is a list of the last mentioned.

England owed its deliverance from the tyrannic yoke of the Danes, to Judith, the stepmother of Alfred.

Philippa of Hainault, the Queen of Edward Third of England, was celebrated for her skill and prudence in military affairs.

The women were foremost in the fifteenth and sixteenth centuries in Hungary, the islands of the Archipelago and the Mediterranean in resisting the aggressions of the Turks.

Ancient history furnishes splendid instances of woman's heroism in defence of country and religion, in the mediaeval ages. There were also many brave warlike women in the French revolution, and in the Peninsular War. In the revolution of 1789 the women of Paris were the foremost actors as actual combatants. The women marched on Versailles to bring back the King of France to Paris. During the campaign of the army of Republican France, under Dumouriez on the Sambre and the Meuse in 1793, Theophile and Felicité Fernig, the daughters of Mortagne, fought at the head of Philippe Egalité's columns, as they had previously, at Valmy, the noisiest battle on record.

Augustina Saragossa, a Spanish woman, called the "Maid of Saragossa," during the Spanish war of independence in the Peninsula, at the time that the most exposed battery had been silenced by the men having been killed, sprang over the dead and dying, snatched a match from a dead artilleryman, fired off a twenty-six pounder, and made a vow not to quit it alive during the siege, and she so inspired the men that the French were repulsed with great loss.

The Helvetian lady warriors are praised by Caesar, in his Commentaries on the Gallic war. More than once have the Roman soldiers fled from the women soldiers of Switzerland.

According to the testimony of Tacitus, a Queen of the ancient Britons led her armies to battle. There were women warriors in her army. During the crusade, many women died with arms in their hands, fighting with other soldiers by their side.

Joan of Arc, the Maid of Orleans, and Joan of Montford, and the celebrated Margaret of Anjou, *all* were as brave as ever *men* were.

Boadicca or Bunduca, the Queen of the Iceni, resisted with her armies, and that in person, the legions of Rome, in the fiercest and most deadly conflicts in which that empire ever engaged. Ethelfreda, the eldest daughter of Peter the Great, commanded armies and gained victories. Renée Bordereau, whose father was butchered before her eyes, and who lost forty-two relatives in the civil war of La Vendée; during the course of six years fought in more than two hundred battles, on foot and on horseback, with the most determined intrepidity. In *one* battle she killed twenty-one of the enemy. She liberated fifty priests at one time and eight hundred at another, all of whom would have been executed. A price of 40,000 francs was set on her head. She was thrown into prison for a crime for which she could only prove her innocence by a discovery of her sex, where she remained five years, until the accession of Louis Eighteenth to the throne of France.

The King of Dahomey has a National Guard that is composed entirely of women, numbering 5,000.

Ex-Queen Isabella of Spain at one time went with her soldiers into her revolted states and entirely quieted them.

About 720 years since, the Moors sought to regain Tortosa, and for a length of time the male inhabitants bore the siege firmly and with the utmost bravery; but after having suffered extreme privations, and every hope had vanished, and they had proposed to yield to the Moors, the women attired themselves in men's clothes and made a resolute sally upon their enemies, with such heroism, that they were compelled to raise the siege, and the Tortosa women returned triumphant to their city, while the Moors fled in dismay and made no further attempt upon Tortosa. For the same, Don Raymond instituted an order of knighthood, in which none but these brave women were admitted. He also ordained that women should be exempt from taxes, and that at all public meetings the women should have the best seats, and that *all* of the apparel and jewels left by their husbands should be lawfully their own. There the women were universally honored and esteemed.

*What of our half Republican country; what of the appreciation of American women? What!*

Men of America—the best and most appreciative of you, will see new charms in woman, or at least you will have an added respect for women generally, when the power of the Ballot is in their hands; as surely as you feel thus towards an enfranchised foreigner with elegance of manners, cultured mind, and well filled purse. With all the above advantages—the wealth, education, elegant appearance and the position that they give—you feel that all are but toys to a *man-resident* of America, if the power of the Ballot is wanting, although he is as well protected as women. There is a feeling that he is something less than yourselves, although he may be superior to you in all things else.

Power always carries with it a certain amount of respect, whether it be of brain, body, purse, or Ballot. But to a native of a Republican country, there must ever be a feeling of insecurity, it matters not how much of all other powers one has, if deprived of *the Ballot, the real birthright of every American child.*

Men of America—you have robbed us of our most precious inheritance—you have robbed us of what you feel a necessity to your protection, with all your superior physical strength. Because we are weaker physically than you, is an incontrovertible reason why we should have what *you* deem the greatest protection to person, property and liberty. That you are our *protectors*, is not true; for if you were, who would there be to protect us from? That you are our *providers*, is equally false, for there are over a million of women in these United States that are toiling early and late in shops, and factories, and garrets, to keep soul and body together—a body half clothed and half starved, and an equally famished soul that weary hours of toil, and half or quarter pay, prevent the possibility of ablutions and clean clothes for the soul!

You would spend the last dime you have; you would spill your last drop of blood before you would see your sons causelessly disfranchised! And yet you lie quietly and unconcernedly down and die, without one thought about your disfranchised daughters. You believe that their husbands will be their protectors, providers, law-makers, and in a word, all that they will be for themselves when they are full fledged citizens in *reality*—you trust all this to a man that you would not to-morrow dare to trust your filthy lucre with! Your daughter's *all*, is in the hands of a man, while she is *deprived* of the Ballot, while you would not, with your superior strength, trust *your* all in his hands, even *with* the power of the Ballot. That man with daughters, who does not labor for their enfranchisement, is unworthy of the name father, and ought to be classed with the senseless fops, or the poor unfortunate old bachelors, whose paternal love has never been awakened.

Men—I need not tell you that the burning facts are the same, "whether you hear, or whether you forbear"—but the *results* are in your hands, for you have the Ballot yourselves, and withhold it from women.

To say that "women shall have it when they ask in mass," is as inconsistent as to say that children shall be clothed and educated when they come on their bended knees and pray to you for such essentials. If you *are* so much the superiors of women, why do you wait for them to ask you for protecting power? If they are so ignorant that they do not see the necessity for such protection, treat them as children and give it to them, and teach them its value and use. If it is not best for them to have such power, why do you promise it, as soon as a certain number express a desire for it? Is a right inherited by all, and desired but by few, any the less a right *now*, than it will be when *all* see its uses? Will a large number possessing an advantage in itself wrong, make that right, which would not be, if exercised by a few?

If I am talking *instinctively*, you must listen and act; for you say *instinct* does not err. But if I am *reasoning* the cause, do not show your want of the power to cope with me, by your anger, but come up like *men* and acknowledge the truth, or bring arguments from your master minds to prove what you in your *sphere* are able to do. Through the power of brute force I see the ballot in your hands, but through the telescope of *justice* I see *woman* having it, is equally certain.

The zephyrs that shall waft the sounds of joy, to be uttered by woman enfranchised, are already "pluming their wings;" and when that time *shall* arrive, in every State husband and wife will walk side by side, in all the important duties of life, being equals *socially* as well as *politically*. Bickerings will cease, for there will be no more *necessity* for strife; and the marriage relation will be a beautiful friendship, such as Heaven designed it *should be*. Then the great principle that just Governments derive their power from the *consent* of the governed, will be a living one, in our dearly loved America—then it will be a whole Republic in reality, instead of being scarcely a *half* one, as it is to-day.

---

NOTE.—This book was written over a year since, before the Territories of Wyoming and Utah had enfranchised the women; or England had enfranchised the single women who pay taxes.

# CHAPTER VI

# DIVORCE

"Whom God hath joined together let not man put asunder."

No one can believe more firmly than the writer in the sacredness of the marriage relation. And perhaps she would be equally slow to advise any one to flee from *present* ills, to those "we know not of."

There is a difference of opinion, however, as to *whom* God hath joined together, and in *what* that joining consists. God's laws are immutable, and if He ever joins two persons together, no man *can* put them asunder;—they may travel the world over, and have all sorts of temptations presented to them, and still they cannot be separated. It is well known that there have been some such cases, examples of which stand out beautifully in bold relief, on the great panorama of ill-assorted marriages.

Nero, the Roman emperor, so envied such a couple that came under his observation, that he ordered them to kill *themselves*; Aria took the fatal knife and stabbed herself, exclaiming "Paetus, *it is not painful.*" The husband immediately followed her example, and those whom "God had joined together," entered the beautiful city of eternity, as Aria and Paetus, the joined on earth, that were beyond the power of being separated in Heaven.

Damon and Pythias were also examples of a "joining" of souls. It was stronger than ties of consanguinity, and stronger than marriage contracts. True marriage of an exalted type must have just *such* a joining as these men had, and then the word *Divorce* can never be found in the lexicon of their hearts.

But there *are* those who have about as correct ideas of noble marriage, as "the cattle on a thousand hills." Some people look upon the institution *only* in a physical light, and live it out on this plan, marrying persons who are widely different. Their *souls* are soon divorced, and then how inhumanly cruel to *compel them by law* to live together! God never "joined" them, and if one of man's enactments is more wicked than another, it is the *compelling* them to live together, when at least *one* of their *souls* is crushed, and one of their *bodies* tormented.

There are various types of "what God has joined together," and also a very wide range of difference in the character of the highest and the lowest of these types. The highest are of the Damon and Pythias order; where the souls are in harmony, each thinking and feeling alike when both understand alike. Not that one is the mental *tool* of the other, but that they are joined by indissoluble ties, which each recognizes in the other, without either feeling placed in a servile position. Divorce laws are no more needed for such, than are extra wings for the dove.

The lowest type of "what God hath joined together," is where there are little minds. Divorces are not needed for such, and they are astonished that any one can be so *wicked* as to allow themselves to *sin* in this direction. From their own stand-point do they judge, and *to* them is their judgment righteous, on the ground that "as a man *thinketh* so *is* he."

We have spoken of but a very small number of the great army of earth's soldiery, who are enlisted in the life battles of marriage. We have only reviewed in your presence, two of the regiments that have never been under fire; but we shall not deceive you into joining the army under false pretences, but take you to a vast battle-field, where the wounded are groaning and the silent sick are in the background in hospitals. The one class are dying slowly but surely, breathing their quiet prayers to Him who hears the gentlest zephyr. The great throng see not the insupportable anguish that the forced smiles cover, and only now and then does a sympathizing heart look in and exclaim, O God, could the world but get a glimpse of this quiet martyrdom, before it is too late! But they cannot believe this sight unless they see it, and they *will* not look!

They turn to the groaners on the field, some of whom joined the army from the highest motives; some because starvation stared them in the face; some because ambitious parents urged them; some because of ennui, and the desire for change; but a large number because public sentiment demanded it, and they entered into the best company there was, in the only regiment that they *could* enlist in, although they were far from being satisfied that it was just *the* place for them.

They look hemp ropes, and daggers, and pistols, and lunatic asylums, and at last exclaim, "You have no *business* to be in such a predicament; it is *your own* fault." "Why did you not join a regiment that would never get into trouble?" "Your getting hurt is plainly your own foolhardiness in not asking everybody's advice." "But you had no *need* of being hurt *any way*; it is the result of indiscretions on your part, and now all your friends must be tortured with the scars upon your face!" "You have disgraced them all, for everybody will hear that you have *been* in the army, and are not in it *now*."

"Ah," cries a poor victim, "trace your own family relations, and you will find that *some* one is in the same condition." Every house in the land has its family record, and its pages are read by outsiders who are often supposed to be ignorant of its secrets, and there are unwritten margins that may *yet* be filled with such as you see before you. See to it that you make such scars in the highest degree honorable, for you know not what hour may find, if not *you*, your children, in an "*action*."

Purity and impurity cannot harmonize. Whenever a George marries a Julia, there is such a wide difference in the depth of purity, and the depth of vice, that whenever the Julia, often viewing the case on every side, decides that the tenderest of affection has lost all power to win from evil, she is untrue to her noble self, if she sins against her highest light, and degrades herself by suffering a George to live with her longer. She can decide for herself with an accuracy that it is impossible for others to understand; and a George who has been leading a dissolute life, will be sure to charge a Julia with coldness, or try to shift the faults of separation off himself, when he has *lost the power* to appreciate sincerity, high-toned purity, and those childish demonstrations of the deepest affection that God has implanted in the human heart.

We have often heard it preached that "a wicked man would be unhappy in heaven." So while a bad individual may feel the loss of the good, and may speak in the most glowing terms of that loss, he is unhappy if obliged to be free from the people with whom he has debased himself. Like the drunkard who has left his cups, or the tobacco-user who sees not the weed, the habits of both mind and body have been such, that nothing but what has been the *cause* of degradation will satisfy, even if a thousand times better in all respects.

But no one who hovers near and undertakes to be a reconciler and unasked adviser, can ever understand such logic, if the knees are bended, and promises made from a smooth tongue, that has made, if possible, falseness one of the component parts of his being. It is not at all a matter of surprise, that such a man should know that a woman who knew him *well*, could never credit promises that she knew were not made to be kept.

The pure always suffer for a time, but that great and beautiful law of adjusting all wrongs *sometime*, at last raises a noble champion, who dares to defend the one who has suffered unwritten agonies, for the sake of eternal principles, which all must understand *sometime*—if not in *this* world, in that which is to come.

How the *want of a Divorce* affects *such*, the farthest range of imagination cannot picture. To be neither married nor single, and be placed in such a position by the delicate facts of the case, that explanations are out of the question in most instances, is what it is literally impossible for any but the noblest and tenderest to comprehend; and hence the want of sympathy for those who thereafter tread life's path *alone*, imparting happiness to others whose sorrows seem almost unendurable.

To be deprived of a Divorce is like being shut up in a prison because some one attempted to kill you. The wicked one takes his ease and continues his *course*, and you take the slanders, without the power to defend yourself. It is just as honorable to get out of matrimonial trouble *legally*, as to be freed from any other wrong. If it is right to be legally married, it is right to be legally Divorced. No one would think of slurring another, who ran out of the reach of a murderer, where simply the "shuffling off this mortal coil" was threatened, but when the God-like principle was being hampered and crushed, and every iota of confidence was literally destroyed, some would censure an individual for freeing *soul* and *body* from such a condition.

It was not until the twelfth century and under the auspices of Pope Innocent Third, that divorces were prohibited by the civil, as well as by the canon law, and it is to be hoped that when the Roman Catholics think more upon the importance of Divorces, (in some cases,) that they will again allow them.

Thanks to an increasing and diffusing sentiment of equity that the breezes of time are fast fanning out such unjust ideas as the right of compelling people to live together when that relation is perfectly agonizing, and all the manufactories of the brain are unable to weave a web of confidence again. One of the most beautiful sayings of our George Washington was in relation to the influence of a bad example on a noble individual, if obliged to remain for a length of time under such influence. And if so in the ordinary relations of life, what shall we say of the *Marriage* relation? Without proper Divorce laws, virtue is robbed of her rights, vice is encouraged, noble aspirations crushed, love turned to hate, and Marriage made wretched beyond the power of human expression.

We recite with all the indignant horror of which we are capable, the wrongs of the ancient Greeks, Jews, and Romans, where they compelled the people by law to marry, and then, no matter how wretched that relation proved to be to the *wives*, there were no Divorce laws for *their* benefit; and yet in our own country, and in our own time, the greatest of outrages imaginable are inflicted without the power to be Divorced from the oppressor.

Thousands of sorrows are brooded over in silence,

when no mortal eye witnesseth the same—thousands of sighs escape the lips, unheard, by mortal ears. ★ ★ ★

But all wrongs come up before the "Great I Am," and Agitators are sent forth to show to the good of earth, their duties to humanity, and strength is given such, to work until justice shall be meted out to all, and the oppressed allowed to go free.

How long, O Lord, how long, must there be such martyrs as the noble Sage, and the sainted Richardson!

# CHAPTER VII

# LABOR

"By the sweat of thy brow, shalt thou eat thy bread."

To remain in absolute idleness, is, to say the least, a great piece of selfishness. Nowhere in life does it seem so glaringly displayed as in cases where a husband is laboring from earliest dawn until latest even, and his wife doing nothing but dressing for dinner parties, making and receiving calls. No matter whether the husband be a professional man, or is extensively engaged in mercantile pursuits, or in any branch of business where the profits are large, sooner or later, if he does not need a helping hand in his wife to save, or retrieve from ruin, he needs sympathy and encouragement, which an idle butterfly wife cannot give. Her living such a life detracts from her character, and, instead of becoming better, truer, and nobler, she is constantly becoming, if not "beautifully less," *a sort of less*, that lessens one's esteem for her.

The mind is either becoming more majestic and beautiful, or it is being dwarfed, as life wears away. Labor of some kind is just as much a necessity to the abiding happiness, as is bread to the existence. The years are not distant, when the truth of this will be realized by every human being.

The following couplet is being acknowledged more and more every year, by our most intelligent people: "Toil of the brain, of the heart, or of the hand, is the only true manhood, the only true nobility." But we would add a word and say, the only true *womanhood* also, and then we would add a line, and have it read—"And the only sure road to happiness."

No kind of Labor should be despised. It is a great piece of human presumption, to say that any part of God's creation in the great field of Labor, is in any way unworthy of your *superior* consideration, when Deity takes cognizance of the smallest Labors performed by mortals, and gives credit for even the handing of a cup of cold water.

If you have a regard for the Bible, you must not forget that your very thoughts are sinful, if indulged in, in relation to sinful matters; if you style and feel yourself above another mortal, simply because he is obeying the command, "do what thy hands find to do," you cannot be guiltless.

The shoddyocracy who despise Labor, and teach their children to do so, are more frequently than otherwise, found to be, at length, lamenting over their children's prodigality, if not absolute viciousness. Thus the marriage relation is embittered, when, if the children had all been educated to perform some kind of Labor, and had had the principles of the *dignity* of the same instilled into their minds, they would have become useful members of society instead of drones, or butterflies, or criminals.

No individuals can occupy any positions of trust, without Labor, if they discharge their duties properly; for they toil with the pen and brain in signing and considering measures, just as much as the mechanic who makes the table the paper rests upon, or the manufacturer who makes the paper; and the ruler, whoever it may be, performs no higher service in writing yes or no than the writer in *speaking* of such persons. The one who tills the soil to raise my food, and the one who cooks the same, helps to give me the use of my brains as effectually as though they guided my hands in writing this book.

If both husband and wife labor according to their abilities, they would not only help to give use to each other's brains, but there would be ample time for each to use his or her own brain, for the good of themselves, and society, and they would both be happier than if either were idle.

Not only every *son*, but every *daughter* should be given a practical knowledge of some business, whereby they can support themselves. It matters not how much wealth there may be in the family, or how high their position is before the world. Wealth "takes wings and flies away;" positions, sometimes, end on desolate isles, where life drags out very wearily. But *whoever* they are, whether inhabitants of palaces, or of hovels, wherever all in the family are laboring a part of the day with brain, heart, or hand, they feel that they are living for some purpose, and that there is some happiness in life.

There are more vacant chairs in family circles, made such by sickness and death, from the system having been worn out endeavoring to gain pleasure, than there are honestly *laboring* to deserve it. The one class spend their days in severe toil, laboring so hard to gain the necessities of existence that the system is constantly overtaxed; the other pass their nights in fashionable follies, and their days in ennui. (Ask the latter class, what has Labor to do with the happiness of the married relation?) Such people are not contented and happy anywhere, and can never sing with the spirit, "Home, sweet home." But the "woman who is kept," feels the sentiment *about* as much, as the one who "marries for the purpose of being supported in idleness;" and while the one despises the other, the question might be raised as to the vastness of the difference of the sins, in the sight of Heaven. Both classes of women would be married, and both respecting themselves *in* marriage, were it not for their dependence on the Labor of men.

A public sentiment that endorses some kinds of Labor as being respectable, and others as *not*; some people as respectable *in* laboring and others as not; that pays to a man's hand twice or thrice as much as a woman's, for the same Labor, performed as well, and in the same length of time, is a part of the chippings of barbarism, that have not yet been hewn off the pillars of civilization. But the axe is already being forged, with edge so keen, that the work will be thoroughly accomplished, long ere the writer shall count her three score years.

The effects of the Labor question are seen in the family relation on every hand, and when "the good time coming" comes, no one will be obliged to Labor more than three or four hours per day, because *all* will Labor as a pleasure *and* a profit to *body* and *mind*, if not for pecuniary reasons. The toiling millions and the idle thousands will then be nearer on a par mentally, because the former will have more time for intellectual improvement, when the body is not so weary with toil, that they cannot appreciate anything but physical necessities.

Ye who have the capital, and oppress the laborers, forget that it is the "talent that you must account for" in the future state of existence. If you oppress them *here*, and prevent them from preparing their minds for an intellectual *hereafter*, you must suffer *there*, by keeping the company of those who are *so* undeveloped, that they are not fitted to be of much service in the great eternity of progression. They are not illiterate, they are not ill-natured, simply because they *prefer* to be, but, because of the unequal distribution of capital, that must always be as it is, until those engaged in the different branches of work are well paid, that they can have time and means for improvement and for rest.

At the present time, not a family exists, where the marriage relation is not affected injuriously, either by the *want* of Labor, or by excessive Labor! The great mass of *wives* are overworked in their homes, "trying to get along without any help, to save expense," when, if the laboring man obtained better wages, the wife could have help constantly. The laboring women are over worked everywhere, as well as the laboring men, but the women are worse off, because of the pittance paid for woman's work.

Thousands of unsuitable marriages are contracted every year, which would never have been, had not the question of Labor been involved. There are but few avocations where women can earn means to purchase homes for themselves, so they do the best they can in getting a permanent shelter by marrying, or "doing worse," and afterwards being diseased and deserted; whereas if the great question of equal pay for work, and good pay at that, and only a few hours per day, were in vogue, they could have a purse of their own, and would not marry until the *really* congenial one was at hand, and a new dress, or a "love of a bonnet," would not be made a temptation to evil, when such clothes were an absolute necessity, in order to keep a respectable room, or remain in respectable company.

Mrs. Crowe has truthfully said, "Few women marry from affection. It is because it is a suitable person." Parents do not wish their daughters to spend their lives with them, unless it be one who can pay her way with Labor of some kind. Grown girls are almost turned out of doors into marriage, by having their destiny as *somebody's* wife constantly preached. Fathers are heard to say that, "daughters are only a bill of expense—if you had been sons, I might have been rich."

Women, in some positions of life, are kept out of marriage because their friends will not consent to their marrying what is usually termed a Laboring man—in others, because they are so worn out with Labor, that they are not *fit* to marry. This is true of the great mass of women in school-rooms, sewing-rooms, and in the various factories and binderies.

While many men retire from business, who ever heard of a *women's retiring from business*, because she had accumulated a competency. Women retire from the school-room, or the clerk's desk, from their six or seven hours per day labors, into the Marriage relation, where their family labors and cares give them only as many hours of rest. Or they retire from the fryingpans of other people's kitchens into the fires of their husbands', when, if they had been properly compensated for their labor before Marriage, they would have saved money enough to have paid others, and not be obliged to labor so hard themselves.

As a rule, that labor which costs the most time, and physical strength, is the most poorly paid, and is usually of a nature that is absolutely essential to existence, or, at least, the common comforts of life. This fact is poignantly felt in the marriage relation, by the toiling wife, who feels that nobody with tender care brushes the great drops of perspiration from her brow, with an appreciating look and with words of encouragement, that helps so much to make the thousand trials of domestic wifehood endurable. The terrible sorrows and discouragemnts, because of not being appreciated, is felt in thousands of homes, both high and low.

The wife who studies from day to day about the kind of food to be prepared, that will be the *best*, with the *least expense*; who performs all the work herself, in kitchen, laundry, nursery and chamber, and then does her sewing by artificial light, sighs over a want of appreciation, and want of time for rest. So does the wife who for long years has directed a number of servants, in *her* large house with its thousand cares and annoyances that hirelings always make, and independent positions always have as accompaniments. Such a one said in conversation with the writer, "Ten years since, my husband retired from business, and has had no cares since, while I have as many as ever."—I believe that when a husband retires from his business to spend the rest of his life in reading and recreation, it is time that his wife retires from housekeeping. His whims of diet, and his vanities of style were as great as ever, and he never for a moment thought that his wife's cares were of much importance, but what they were, must be according to the "sphere" that God *intended* for woman. In such thoughts, he is no better and no worse than the great mass of men, who underrate the work of woman in the family relation.

Sons, as well as daughters, should be brought up to learn the complicated duties of housekeeping. Everything about the kitchen, dining-room, laundry, parlor, making and mending of clothes—in a word, everything that is considered woman's peculiar duties, should be and must be thoroughly learned by boys, before such Labors and duties will ever be appreciated by men.

One, and I may say the great reason, why the mass of

women are so dissatisfied with their domestic duties, is because they are painfully conscious of the inability of men to duly appreciate the thousand cares, thoughts, and anxieties of their position. Too well do women know that the great mass of men feel that if they *earn* the money, they have performed the nine-tenth part of living, and whatever a woman does is only of minor consideration; and thinking this, men act it in a way that pains and discourages women.

All woman's reasoning of the case goes for naught, because (not that men intend to be unjust to women, not that they intend to make them feel that they are, and *must ever be*, under a tied-up sort of obligation to them for home and shelter, but) it is perfectly impossible for men to realize what is due to woman, unless they have, at some period of life, had a practical knowledge of what a woman's duties are.

There are times and occasions in the life of nearly every man when all of such knowledge is of the greatest of importance to men, as regards *comfort* if not *economy*, when the mother or the wife is sick. How much lighter would the broom and smoothing-irons seem if women knew that they had been used by men who had left a touch of appreciation upon them. How much less oppressive would the cook stove seem, if women knew that men's brains had been heated to agony over it; not that "misery loves company," but that every human being loves appreciation, and everybody knows that no one can fully appreciate what they have not known practically.

It is no wonder that men are so unsympathizing and

unappreciating, when they are so practically ignorant of what they ought to know. The long tirades about "woman's duties" and "woman's spheres" will be wonderfully shortened when men learn *all* of the duties of *their* spheres, the most important of which, is the domestic—(when woman is necessarily taken out of it by maternal sickness) who so blind that they will not see that everything that has before devolved on the wife, now is left entirely to the husband, or *should be*, to facilitate her recovery.

But we would not take from men credit that is due to them, for there *are women* who do not appreciate the labors of men, and who do not use money judiciously, and who never feel at all grateful for money that they have neither helped to save, nor encouraged in earning. Such are few, however, and when the toils of the marriage relation are more equally divided and the respectability of all kinds of Labor fully established, the good effects of such a system will be seen in there being few who are unmarried, and much more genuine love in the marriage relation.

But a great work is yet to be accomplished, for "one half of the world knows nothing about the other half" and are not prepared to sympathize with them, for they do not know there are so many groaning beneath Labor chains.

Those who toil excessively become so weary that the rare and beautiful gems of thought, that they try to save in their memory (until they can command *time to write them down,*) break and vanish like air bubbles, and no one will believe they were ever *thought*, because they never saw any evidence of their having had an existence.

Some of their thoughts are as much more beautiful than those who have ample time to express them well, as are the air bubbles from the pipe of a child, more perfect and beautiful, than the real balloon of the man.

Who will say that the marriage relation would not be made much happier, if the Laborers had time to think and write? for as it affords *me* happiness in expressing my ideas, and makes *me* more noble, so it would another human being. Every noble expression adds a *title* to one's own soul's nobility.

There are branches of Labor where one cannot stop and pen the burning words, that *rush out of the brain*, and demand paper to rest upon, and a pen to hold them there. But if they labored a fewer number of hours, had better pay for Labor, they would not be so weary that they would forget how to clothe their beautiful ideas, or where they last saw the naked truths that begged for apparel. Many a laborer has listened to such appeals, with a sorrowing heart, knowing that his or her want of time to clothe, would result in the interment of the neglected gems, and they could only attend the funeral, for that takes but *little time*, and so everybody can attend funerals. The immortal Tupper, in the following words, has beautifully expressed the necessity for clothing the "naked" ideas as soon as they are called for.

"Hast thou a thought upon thy brain?
Catch it ere it fly,
Or other thoughts will intervene,
And it will soon take wing."

We predict that the time *will* come, when there will be *time* for all Laborers to heed his advice; for they will not consume so many hours in work, but that if their thoughts *do* take wing, they can keep sight of them, and overtake them at last without the use of a velocipede. That the Laborers do not desire more time for intellectual pursuits, and are incapable of appreciating and enjoying a higher culture, is a piece of that book of sophistry, from which we have heard so many quotations, that we are led to believe that many people express themselves not only ignorantly, but thoughtlessly.

The great mass of the manual Laborers of our country, can comprehend whatever profound reasoning may be brought before them. And who will pretend that the mind that can *understand* is not as great, *naturally*, as the one that can create? The only difference is in the power of surroundings that have developed the one into *expressing* what the other would have been able to do, if as well informed.

Those who would keep a certain class in ignorance, for the purpose of being almost revered for their own lore and positions, forget that the higher the culture, the greater the appreciation, and as a natural consequence, the better the people and the better the marriage relation generally. That there *always* will be *some* who are grovelling, and half idiotic, or for many hundreds of years, no one will doubt; but such, in time, will be looked upon with that same kind of pity, that their deplorable conditions shall elicit from the truly noble of earth.

Would not the marriage relation be bettered if such

were kept in asylums, and not allowed to marry and entail their wretched condition on offsprings, whose chances of becoming respectable and intelligent citizens were still less than their parents?

If half grown children in filthy streets, who are growing up in idleness, were taken to asylums where they could be taught trades, and educated for the ordinary business of life, they would not live in such filth afterwards, and the habits of neatness that would be acquired would be carried into homes of their own. Both sexes should be treated in this way, and parents not allowed to visit them, unless they were sober and cleanly in their appearance.

Our free schools do not accomplish all that was hoped for the lowest classes, and there is an absolute neccssity for other educational advantages which cannot be given them in a systematic manner, unless they are under the control of those who make a business of teaching practical as well as theoretical ideas. The cost of such institutions to the State, would not be as great as the policemen's salaries to watch their filthy dens, and the costs of Jails and Courts.

In time the marriage relation of such would be made much better; for, if the parents would not live soberly and respectably, their children would be away from such influences, and would never settle down into their parents' degrading style of *existing* when, by proper Labor, they could live comfortably, and well.

Better classes suffer in consequence of the wrongs of the Labor question. Many would have been married who are now living in a most wretched condition, having no homes, and never can have, because the pay for their labor is so small. They cannot accumulate a sufficient amount before marriage to warrant them in assuming the responsibilities of the relation, which, in the first place, calls for a house, or a high price for board. It has been said, and too truthfully, that the first years of married life are either commenced in an extravagant way, so that in a few years they are obliged to strain every nerve, simply to live respectably and keep up an appearance, or are obliged to go to some new country, and be prisoners half of a lifetime, and thus their minds are dwarfed by hard Labor, and want of time to improve the mental condition.

No individuals can be entirely absorbed in excessive physical toil, without detracting from the mental powers. You can see, as you go to a country church, who are overworked through the week, by the head's dropping, and the arms of Morpheus at once encircling the listener. However interesting the speech, it is impossible for the tired body to allow the mind to comprehend all that is said, and the mind is so tired *with* the body, that it cannot think clearly on any subject whatever. Look at the effect on the children of such overworked parents! It must be evident that the mind of such cannot be as thoroughly developed as though they had time for recreation and mental improvement. There is much truth in the assertion, "where no bread is brought in at the door, love goes out of the window," and it needs but little observation to see that love can not feed on air, and that minds of parents can not feed on air either, and manufacture brains to give to posterity. That there are a great many unhappy hours caused by the poverty in many poor families is too true. The husband is too weary to attend lectures, and besides he cannot afford to spend a dollar not strictly necessary, and thus a great and important source of, not only recreation, but of improvement is lost.

Many a soul is hemmed and packed and compressed into a narrow life, with pure and extensive aspirations. Many a great soul yields quietly to conditions that *are*, wearing out the body in but partially requited toil, that irritates the nervous system to such an extent, that the effects on the marriage relation are far from being happifying.

I am ashamed of so much of our American boasting, when I look facts in the face, and hear the unsung agonies of thousands of our people, that toil all their lives, and die without owning a little home. They nestle into the bosom of our mother Earth, feeling that *somebody* had deprived them of a cot, or a foot of land.

Away in the distant future, the people of the day will charge the great land-owners, and stock-owners, and *great everybodies*, with selfishness unparalleled, when they read that many fathers never saw any of their children by daylight, except on Sunday, as they were all day at work in factories, mines and railroads, and that many husbands and fathers never saw their wives and children in the beautiful light of day, because so weary on Sundays, after the long week's Labors, that they could not keep their own eyes open to *look at them*!

It is strange, when all the comforts and luxuries enjoyable are produced by Laboring people, that the wealthy do not make greater efforts to show appreciation of the Laborers! It is only when there is a colliery explosion, that the dangers which attend the digging of coal to make us comfortable in cold weather, seem to be realized. It is only when a switch tender fails in his duty, and a collision of railroad coaches results, that we realize (as the mangled masses of humanity are before us) how dependent we are upon the Labor of the men who graded the road, the men who made the track, the men who laid the rails, the men who made the comfortable coaches, with cushioned seats, looking-glasses, stoves with glowing fires, and all the comforts of travel.

Not one luxurious couch, not one magnificent mirror, not one splendid carpet, not one marble-top table, but that, for style and beauty, we owe not only to the *hands*, but to the conceptions of beauty, and utility of the poor Laborer. Not one exquisitely wrought silver dish upon your mahogany dining-table, or even the brilliant flowers in your vases, but that cost the hard, and poorly paid toil of workers that are unnoticed by you. Even the linen in its snowy whiteness that you sleep upon, and wear in displaying your diamonds, are brought to you by woman's blistered hands, that you pay so poorly for the toil that causes the suffering! It is not only her *hands*, but her soul's anxiety to have the clothes suit, that helps to wear *her* life, and use up *her* strength, and yet no one seems to think that there is anything but *physical* toil with the laundry woman.

The happiness of the marriage relation everywhere would be enhanced, if all were paid better for their Labor, worked a fewer number of hours in a day, and were duly appreciated in the performance of the same, and were made to feel, that, as it was noble for Deity to Labor and make the Heavens and the Earth, and all that in them is, "it is noble for His creatures, one and all, to do what their hands find to do."

# CHAPTER VIII

# RELIGION

In every human heart some Religious emotions are to be found. There is a consciousness of the existence of a power higher than oneself; and the fact of such superiority, calls forth respect, reverence, worship. But all of these emotions must *first* be felt towards a mortal, and the more intense they are towards the human, the greater they will be when years and reason bids them look higher.

The father and mother is the God in the eyes of the little child, for it knows of nothing higher, with its infantile reason. We are surprised when we think how differently minds view the attributes of Deity, and yet it is not so wonderful after all, when we study the subject and realize that the parents or the guardians make the ideas of the character of Deity, in the future mature individual.

In the tender years of the child, if the rulings are in love and kindness, and the parents' acts before the child are of the same character, the child will form an idea of God as an all loving Father, seeking the best good of His children, and the chastisements will seem to come from such loving hands, that the pain will all be in the realization of the fact, that a wrong has been committed, or a duty neglected; and there will not need to be any sermons for the purpose of showing the importance of innumerable resolves being made to live a better life in future.

But on the other hand, if the parents are unkind, exacting, assuming, and tyrannical towards the child, having no mercy or justice in dealing with little faults, and utter ignorance, the child will have an idea of a God that is filled with anger, bottled up against a day of impulsive wrath, that shall frighten one into a hope of sinking out of existence in eternity, if there be an annihilation to get to, after we find the eternal shores of the last and final settling up of our earthly accounts, that are written in the great book of His remembrance.

The child with the former training and under the love-to-do-right influence, because it *is* right, is a thousand times better to its parents, than one with the latter harsh and tyrannical ideas, who must all through life look upon the parents as masters instead of friends; and upon God as the great master and tyrant, that rules with a rod of iron in *this* world, and burns with fire and brimstone in the world to come, where the fire can never be quenched, and where Deity and saints will glory over their eternal agonies.

Indeed, earthly parents have been known to expend all the fury from hands and tongue upon their children, that they dared to do, and then finish up with the representation of a lake of literal fire and brimstone, into which they will be hurled after death by God.

Such parents are most unhappy themselves, and seem not to be able to live without making their children wretched, and so such children go forth and commit all sorts of crimes, with a stolid indifference to consequences, believing that there cannot be a greater Hell *out* of this life, than there is in it.

Religion has something that is *telling*, to do with the marriage relation, when such results proceed from the Religious teachings of parents, whether they fill pulpits or groggeries.

Parents that teach their children that the most beautiful part of Religion is the golden rule of the Christ, that so beautifully taught the love principles to God and man, will in turn find the same reflected back upon themselves, and the great humanity, to which we are all under obligations to love as did Christ, and not to turn away with, "be ye fed and be ye clothed," and be ye loved and encouraged, by somebody, but not by us.

No one subject has been discussed by all the world, (where the people have been allowed to think for themselves,) that has produced so much inharmony in the marriage relation as the subject of Religion.

It would seem, that, when there are such a variety of opinions on this subject, and the fact so well known that one's Religious belief is sacred to them, that, when married people know their beliefs are different on denominational subjects, and cannot be made to harmonize, that they would never undertake to discuss the subject.

Much of the inharmony of the marriage relation, results from a difference in the Religious sentiments, or rather the doctrinal points, as sent forth by leading theologians.

It has been said that "married people can never discuss any subject without getting more or less angry before closing," and this is especially true in Religious discussions, but not because they are *married*, for all people who do not consent to differ upon this subject, without discussion, feel an enmity towards each other.

But if married people quarrel over subjects under discussion, it is because they have more time to discuss than other people; and as woman under the law, has not as many rights as man, she must of necessity avail herself of her weapon of defence that man cannot legislate away from her.

Religion is almost the only subject about which many women dare to differ from their husbands, whenever a discussion closes.

There is more of intolerance manifested upon this subject than any in the world, and yet here and there, the wife, who is so timid in calling forth a dissent to her ideas on other topics, comes out boldly and makes her own assertions of belief, as if she were really entitled to such expression—as if she had a right to "her say," as a distinct human intelligence.

An advantage is taken of the subject, and a woman is

the supreme controller of her own ideas, and *will have her will*, in their expression. The husband submits because the wife has the advantage, but this compulsory submission does not always make him any more amiable than he often sees his wife, after other discussions, where by browbeating or by physical force, *he* has gained the victory.

It is assuming much more than is modest, to say the least, to expect because two persons enter into the marriage relation, that they ought, or will be likely, to think alike on a subject that the wisest, those who have made theology a special study, differ so widely upon.

As there is something good in all Religious beliefs, there should be a quiet toleration towards all who represent the various forms or ceremonies that are connected with worship. No misrepresentations of the Bible on the inferiority of sex, can ever produce any happiness in the Religious world, any more than elsewhere, and any sect that advocates such a theory, must sooner or later lose all of its intelligent and respectable members. If there is a necessity for men to be active in Religion, there is the same necessity for women, and the same obligation. Hundreds of married people have lived wretchedly and finally separated, in consequence of an advantage having been taken of the writings of Paul as explained in some of our churches.

It is a terrible fact, that there are more quarrels in families on account of the misconstruction of Paul's writings, than any one cause, and among Religious people, I do not know but I am warranted in saying, any combination of causes. Many women have left the church, because they felt their womanhood so degraded by the teachings on this subject.

There is no doubt that the women of Hindostan feel the same kind of degradation, when they are compelled to carry out the Religious rites of wife-burning on the funeral pile of husbands.

Men are startled at such comparisons, but thousands of women, even in our churches, would be willing to endure Hindostan martyrdom, at their husbands' funeral, if they could but escape the terrible wrongs that are endured during their lives.

Any Religion that gives the wife a servile position, is beneath the great plans of Deity, and must ultimately be considered one of the tokens of barbarism, that Christ tried to exterminate, by teaching the beautiful golden rule. Unless women in all the churches are elevated to their true positions, as companions of men, and not treated in any way as Religious inferiors, the sects that persist in wrongs of this character, will, sooner or later, be swept out of the Religious world; for the beautiful refining, and purifying influences of Religion, were not designed to make women wretched; and everything that has a disturbing or unharmonious effect must be removed.

Both men and women have been martyrized in ages past, for daring to think upon Religious matters differently from those belonging to national churches. But thanks to the sun of progress that is shining brighter and brighter every age, drying up the mists of superstition and intolerance, with which the atmosphere of our loving Father has been filled.

Every age brings with it a clearer view of Him who has been hid by this mist, and ere long we may hope that the masses will see the King of Kings in a pure and glorious light, and point their little ones to Him, as their dearest friend, and not as a tyrant to be feared.

Since the days when men and women were drowned, strangled, and burned, in the old world, because of Religious belief, down to the time of time hanging of Quakers in Massachusetts, for their belief, broader and truer ideas have been so disseminated, that, when we have learned of people being imprisoned in Spain for daring to read the ordinary Testament, and of Mrs. Louisa Jeanson of Sweden being jeered and ill-treated in the streets of Saru, Sweden's fashionable resort, for daring to be a Baptist, instead of belonging to the established church of Lutherans, all through intelligent society, we hold up our hands in horror, and say, is it possible that such things have occurred within the last ten years? And yet we see progress, for Mrs. Jeanson was not tied to a stake, where the tidal waters of a Loch Long would make her a watery grave, nor has a Spaniard been strangled and burned, as was William Tyndale in the days of Henry VIII, about the year 1534, for translating the Testament into English, so that all could read it. Spain is ashamed of her treatment of a Testament reader, and Sweden would not to-day allow any more of ill-treatment because any of its citizens believed in immersion.

The days of golden rules of Religion will surely come, and in the family relation as well as elsewhere, all will believe Religiously, as seemeth to them good, without any one questioning their inalienable right to do so—no one will, in an authoritative manner say—why think ye thus? but all will have a liberty of conscience and of speech, which will be such in reality.

No Religion is true and genuine, it matters not what church its representatives belong to, unless it is something that makes homes happy, and ennobles life generally, by the precepts and examples of Christ, as embodied in the grandeur of the golden rule.

Those Religious sects living out these principles, it matters not by what names they are known to the world, will live as great and noble bodies while time lasts, and will contribute to make the Marriage relations and homes generally, "The dearest places" and conditions on earth.

## THE END

* 9 7 8 1 5 3 8 1 7 8 3 3 1 *